Greece & Rome

NEW SURVEYS IN THE CLASSICS No. 19

SLAVERY

BY

T. E. J. WIEDEMANN

WITH ADDENDA (1992)

Published for the Classical Association

OXFORD UNIVERSITY PRESS

Oxford University Press, Walton Street, Oxford OX2 6DP

OXFORD NEW YORK TORONTO
DELHI BOMBAY CALCUTTA MADRAS KARACHI
PETALING JAYA SINGAPORE HONG KONG TOKYO
NAIROBI DAR ES SALAAM CAPE TOWN
MELBOURNE AUCKLAND

AND ASSOCIATED COMPANIES IN
BEIRUT BERLIN IBADAN NICOSIA

ISBN 0 903035 48 0

First published 1987
Reprinted with Addenda 1992

Printed in Great Britain
by Bell and Bain Ltd.,
Glasgow

CONTENTS

LIST OF ILLUSTRATIONS

1. A slave massages his master's foot: Euphronios Crater, 5th c. BC (courtesy Antikenmuseum, Staatliche Museen, Preussischer Kulturbesitz Berlin).

2. A slave girl with cropped hair holds a box for her mistress: black figure lekythos, 5th c. BC (courtesy Musées Royaux d'art et d'histoire, Brussels, inv. 1019; photo ACL, Bruxelles).

3. Tombstone of a child with his *paedagogus*, Athens (Conze, *Attische Grabreliefs* (Vienna, 1893 ff.), No. 878). Drawn by Pam Baldaro.

4. Shackles, presumably for slaves, from the Laureum mines. Ca. 4th c. BC (From the collection of the Bergakademie Freiberg, GDR).

5. Slaves as workers: the exploitation of agricultural slaves in the Roman empire, as depicted in a Soviet school textbook (F. P. Korovkin, *History of the Ancient World* (Moscow, 1962), ill. XII).

6. Slaves as servants: a Roman lady having her hair dressed; from Neumagen (courtesy Rheinisches Landesmuseum, Trier)

7. A Roman manumission ceremony (courtesy Musée Royal de Mariemont, Belgium).

8. The crucifixion of Spartacus (p. 47) (F. P. Korovkin, *History of the Ancient World* (Moscow, 1962), ill. XIV).

I. THE HISTORIOGRAPHICAL ISSUES

The sheer quantity of academic work since the war concerning itself with slavery in the Greek and Roman world reflects the subject's continuing fascination. It makes it impossible for any single person to be aware of all the particular trends in research around the world at the moment, and it makes it necessary for this survey to be very selective in its references to recent studies of particular aspects of the subject.[1]

Many scholars have considered slavery the key to an understanding of what life in the ancient world was like. Needless to say, they have approached it from the standpoint of their own most fundamental preconceptions and value-judgements; and since these basic 'ideological' concerns differ from scholar to scholar, their application to as major a social institution as slavery has made this more controversial a subject than any other in the study of ancient literature and society.

The Heritage of Abolitionism

One of the roots of this special concern with slavery is historical. Only a few generations ago, some of the ancestors of modern Englishmen, Frenchmen, and Americans were involved in slavery, either as slaves or as masters. Until the eighteenth century, slavery as an institution was taken for granted, whether or not it was widespread. Then, quite suddenly, in the second half of the eighteenth century it came to be regarded as a moral evil of a peculiar kind. Abolitionism – referring, in the first place, to the abolition of the slave trade as enacted by the United Kingdom Parliament in 1807, and later to the abolition of slavery itself in Britain's West Indian colonies in 1833 – was perhaps the most important plank in the British radical platform. It appealed not just to fear of the unfair competition that cheap slave labour threatened for the 'free' market of the new industrial Britain, but also to the moral sentiments of the middle classes and of large sections of religiously-minded artisans, labourers, and gentry, even though some contemporaries were well aware how anti-slavery emotions were being exploited to divert attention away from the need for social reform in Britain or Ireland.[2]

Once the Abolitionists had created a climate of opinion in the English-speaking world in which it was taken for granted that slavery was unacceptable in a civilized society, they were faced with the paradox that many societies did not share this view. Sometimes the conclusion was simple: foreigners who practised slavery were just not civilized, and Europeans were justified in using force against them to suppress the slave trade on the High Seas, and slavery itself in India, the Muslim world, and Africa. Coming to terms with the fact that the ancient Greeks and Romans had practised slavery was more difficult. European intellectuals looked to the classical world for paradigms of civilized behaviour. If the ancient Babylonians, Egyptians, or even Jews practised slavery, then that merely showed that these cultures were 'oriental', like those of contemporary Muslims or Hindus. But the societies that produced Greek and Roman literature, philosophy, and law were thought to be at the root of modern European culture. That they should have tolerated slavery was a special problem for those who believed in the Enlightenment and in personal liberty, and in their attempts to come to terms with that problem they and their successors approached Greek and Roman slavery in ways which have often made it more rather than less difficult to understand.

Some of the questions raised in the debate about the moral and economic disadvantages of slavery are no longer taken seriously as academic issues. Was slavery inimical to family ties and sexual morality, thus inhibiting population growth? Did the 'race mixture' brought about by Roman slavery result in an absence of ethnic identity, leading to 'the general creeping paralysis of ancient culture'?[3] Other issues raised then continue to warrant discussion: for instance the proposition that one element of the 'slave mentality' was a lack of interest in, or even a resistance to, technological progress, so that slavery was responsible for the ancient world's failure to 'take off' economically.[4]

The most attractive way of dealing with the embarrassment of ancient slavery was to claim that it had in fact been abolished. Slavery is constantly referred to in the literature, philosophy, and legal writing of antiquity. By comparison, its place in the Christian religious writing of the Middle Ages is minimal. It was easy, but fallacious, to conclude that there was a point where chattel-slavery disappeared and was replaced by medieval serfdom, a form of inequality that did not deny the dependent his humanity. This point could be identified with the 'Fall of the Roman Empire', when Germanic lords with their followers took over political authority from slaveholding Roman senators. The evidence of the survival of slavery throughout the medieval Mediterranean world was simply ignored. For those who were concerned to prove that civilized people could not tolerate slavery, this purported disappearance of the institution from Western Europe in the fifth century A.D. could be interpreted as the culmination of centuries of humanitarian abolitionist effort. Different scholars looked for the abolitionists in different quarters. Secular or rationalist historians saw

developments in Roman law as reflecting an enlightened administration's desire to protect slaves as a first step towards abolition. The
idea that slavery was unknown in 'natural law' but simply an institution of positive law, as it appears in Justinian's *Institutes* (1, 2.2),
was interpreted as a programmatic call for abolition and traced back
to the Sophists Alcidamas and Antiphon in the fifth century B.C.
Abolitionist views were ascribed to Stoic writers, and Seneca's 47th
Letter was celebrated as a particularly fine instance of ancient
humanitarianism. For those who were religiously inclined, it was
Christianity that provided the impetus behind the disappearance of
ancient slavery; quite understandably, since evangelical Protestants
played such a major role in the modern abolitionist movement, and
appealed to scriptural statements about the equality between free and
slave in the eyes of God written by men who lived when Roman
slavery was at its height.[5]

Because Britain, France, and the United States were involved in
slavery and its abolition, the subject evokes peculiar emotions of guilt
and loathing. But the perception that slavery is peculiar amongst
human social institutions is more than just the result of the Western
experience. What makes slavery unique as an unequal relationship is
that it denies the slave any existence as a person independent from
that which his master chooses to grant him. Slavery is an ideal subject
to which to apply the Structuralist concept of 'marginality'. This has
been done with conspicuous success by the American sociologist
Orlando Patterson, who has pointed out that a slave is both physically
alive and socially dead, and that this marginal status has been characteristic of slaves wherever the institution has been practised.[6]

Such 'marginality' is always fascinating. Things that are marginal
are ambivalent, pointing in two directions. This makes the onlooker
uncertain into which conceptual category to place them, and consequently what moral judgements to make and what practical action to
take. What is 'marginal' of course has to be defined with reference to
what is 'central', and different societies may have quite different ideas
as to what should be at the centre of social life: in terms of buildings,
the Cathedral, the Palace, the Parliament, the Stock Exchange or the
Sports Hall. In the Greek and Roman city, it was the *agora* or *forum*,
the meeting-place of free adult male citizens. In a world where the
citizen was at the centre of human activity, slavery represented the
opposite pole of minimum participation in humanity, and the slave
came to symbolize the boundary of social existence. In other societies
where citizenship and the exercise of political rights were not considered essential and central to being human, intellectuals emphasized
different boundaries to full humanity. At various times, people have

used the conceptual image of witches, Jews, Jesuits, blacks, whites, communists, or fascists to help them to arrange their ideas of what is normal, proper, and socially central.

Although this approach has its limitations, it helps us to understand why apparently quite different phenomena are often found in association: shepherds and miners underground, eunuchs and emperors, Negroes and Scythians, share with slaves the quality of being at the edge of humanity. Such marginal phenomena are fascinating for thinkers in any culture. Roman gladiators may be taken as a paradigmatic example (although they did not by any means have to be slaves). These individuals had been condemned to death by their masters or through the courts, and were already in a sense 'dead' when they appeared in the arena ('we who are about to die salute you'); yet they might escape the death to which they had been condemned by performing bravely.[7] Many aspects of Greek and Roman slavery become easier to understand when seen in terms of this sociological model of slavery as 'marginal', between life and death.

Marxism and Mainz

Quantitatively if not qualitatively, the main impetus to the study of ancient slavery over the last hundred years has come from Marxism. In order to evaluate the contribution that Marxist historians have made to the subject, it is necessary to consider the place of slavery in Marxist theory. Starting from the premiss that the conflict of interest between those who provided capital and those who provided labour was central both to an understanding of his own time and to an economic science capable of predicting the future, Karl Marx (1818–1883) went on to suggest that all earlier conflict could similarly be reduced to the opposing interests of pairs of economic classes. Marx's neo-Hegelian model of the human past as a series of conflicts whose resolution leads to a more efficient economic system, bringing with it in its turn new conflicts between classes, has produced some worthwhile historical insights. But Marx was a political activist, not a historian; his remarks about ancient and medieval history are unspecific and often contradictory, and were never meant to constitute a 'system'.[8]

Nevertheless it was from Marx that some of his followers, in particular Engels and then Stalin, derived a rigidly schematic interpretation of human history as consisting of five stages: archaic patriarchal society; ancient slaveholding society; feudalism; capitalism; and finally communism. The vast majority of the population of antiquity was thought to be slaves, and the slaves and 'workers' or 'producers' were held to be identical. During the Stalinist era in the Soviet Union, and after the war in those parts of central Europe and the Balkans which fell under communist control, the main political duty of ancient historians was to demonstrate that slavery lay at the root of every phenomenon of ancient material and cultural life, and to see how the theory of a revolutionary change from an economic system based on the exploitation of slaves to one based on serfdom could be applied to Late Antiquity. In respect of the first of these aims, Marxists in East and West share common ground with others who have seen slaves primarily as an economic class, a group of producers whose labour was exploited by their owners, and with those who have maximized the importance of slavery in the ancient world.[9]

Even if slaves could validly be equated with 'producers' in some of the slave societies of the New World, this certainly did not apply in antiquity. A great deal of productive work was at all times done by people who were not slaves. Smallholders and day-labourers existed even in first-century Italy, when large-scale slavery was once supposed to have monopolized agricultural production. In building, handicrafts, and even mining, free craftsmen are found working alongside slaves.[10] Apart from free citizen labour, many ancient societies had groups of dependent workers whose contribution to agricultural production, and hence to the wealth upon which elite culture was based, was much greater than that of chattel-slaves. The orthodox Stalinist answer was that such servile statuses were all 'slaves' according to the Marxist schema; and indeed the fact that Greek and Roman writers such as Plato when he talked about the Spartan helots or Tacitus in his account of serfdom amongst the ancient Germans were unable or unwilling to distinguish serfs from slaves might seem to support this view.[11]

There were specific reasons why an Athenian or a Roman saw society primarily in terms of the polarity between slaves and free citizens, and either ignored intermediate groups (e.g. Athenian Metics) or labelled them as slaves. We may refer to Patterson's model of slavery as being at the margin of free society. Ancient writers thought a great deal about the concepts 'freedom' and 'slavery', but had little interest in intermediate statuses. This symbolic importance of slavery as the negation of freedom was reinforced by particular historical circumstances. Some of the most important Greek communities formally abolished these intermediate statuses as they developed into constitutional states. Solon's abolition of the *hektēmoroi* ('sixth-sharers') at Athens in ca. 600 B.C. is an example. Later Athenians could only envisage such dependants in the form of debt-bondsmen, free smallholders who had sold themselves to a wealthier neighbour because they had fallen into debt; but the idea of the dependant as 'in debt' towards his lord because he was unable to pay his tithes belongs to a society of formally equal citizens. In archaic Attica, the 'indebtedness' may have been an expression rather than a cause of the relationship of dependence.[12] At Rome too there were restrictions on the exploitation of peasant labour, and enslavement for debt ceased from the fourth century B.C., when the beginning of Rome's wars of conquest resulted in an improved status for peasant soldiers. The consequent clear and sharp distinction between the rights of citizens, no matter how lowly, and the rightlessness of chattel-slaves was codified and reinforced by the development of Roman law, and it left no place for the serfs the Romans came across in Etruria and elsewhere throughout their empire.

To explain the fact that most of the producers whose labour was exploited by the Greek and Roman elite, and by political and clerical elites in ancient India, China, and the Near East, were peasants and not chattel-slaves, Marxists have recently tended to fall back on the concept of an 'Ancient' or 'Asiatic Mode of Production'. The idea originates from Marx's view that while western civilization experienced the paradigmatic economic development from slavery through feudalism to capitalism, other parts of the world had stagnated in a system of exploitation which hampered the development of class consciousness and could thus never undergo the revolutionary transformation into anything more efficient. Stalin found this expression of western superiority congenial when he was imposing Moscow's control over the international communist movement. According to this theory, any culture like the Chinese which found itself in the cul-de-sac of the 'Asiatic' Mode of Production would be unable to achieve socialism independently, but required the leadership of the communist party of a country like Russia which had progressed through all the orthodox stages.[13]

This is not to say that the concept of an 'Ancient' or 'Asiatic Mode of Production' cannot be of some use. The essence of this Mode is held to be that in such societies economic exploitation was a function or result of political or social relationships which were not themselves exclusively economic. Thus in Mesopotamian Temple states, wealth was transferred from the producing peasants to the consuming clerical elite because of the social relation between the two groups (in this case, one based on religion). In classical Athens and Rome, wealth was transferred from subjects or allies to the citizens of the imperial power through war-booty, cleruchies or colonies, tribute, taxes, presents, or bribes: these were all the effects of political relationships,

even if the persons concerned were well aware of the economic consequences of these relationships. On this view, chattel-slavery as practised in the ancient Mediterranean was not a separate type of exploitation: it was merely the most extreme way in which one social
group could use its political power for economic advantage. In recent
years ancient historians even in the Soviet Union itself have revised
the traditional picture to the extent that some of them accept that the
ancient world has to be analysed in terms of social status rather than
economic class, and that the exploitation of inferiors was not primarily
for their labour (since the accumulation of capital was not central to
ancient economics), but for their services.

These developments in Eastern Europe have occurred not just
because of new empirical studies of the ancient world, but also because
of the need to come to terms with ideas about the ancient economy
formulated by 'progressive' western scholars, by no means all of them
orthodox Marxists. The most important of these was undoubtedly Sir
Moses Finley (1912–86). Forced to leave New York in the 1950's as a
result of Senator McCarthy's persecution of 'fellow-travellers', Finley
taught at Cambridge, where he held the Chair of Ancient History between 1970 and 1979. His interest in ancient slavery arose not so
much from the fact that he was a student of W. L. Westermann (who
compiled what remains a standard description of slavery based on the
ancient sources),[14] as from his contact with the European refugees
associated with the 'Frankfurt School' who taught at Columbia University from the 1930's on and spread the ideas of sociologists such as
Max Weber. Weber (1864–1920) was a German nationalist who
stressed the significance of social groups as a corrective to what he
saw as the decadence of English and French liberal individualism.[15]
This emphasis on the primacy of social relations and on the ideological
beliefs held by different status-groups has been seen as an inversion
of the Marxist emphasis on the primacy of economic relations; but
Weber's views can easily be combined with Marxist ideas about pre-
capitalist societies, and scholars associated with the Frankfurt School
such as Karl Polanyi have made considerable contributions to our
understanding of the ancient economy.[16] Finley's ideas about the
ancient economy were within this tradition.[17] For Finley, as for
Weber, the concept of an autonomous 'economy' did not exist in antiquity; hence we must see slaves as a 'status group', not as an economic
'class'; and we must try to understand the economic choices made by
individuals (e.g. to consume services rather than to develop new tech-
nologies) in terms, not of the profit-maximizing economic rationalism
imposed by capitalism, but of the specific and equally rational priorities dictated by the 'mentality' or 'value system' of the social group to

which the individual belonged. It has been a matter of real concern to some communist scholars whether Finley's views qualify as truly Marxist.[18] Whether or not this matters, it illustrates the influence of Finley's approach to slavery amongst academic ancient historians working in a neo-Marxist milieu. This influence can most clearly be seen in the papers presented at a series of informal colloquia on slavery and other aspects of ancient social history over the last fifteen years, initially held at Besançon[19] and, as Heinz Kreissig (1921–84), the East German historian of the Ancient Near East, reported, 'witnessing to the great interest which the theory of the progressive stages of economic social formations and, within that framework, the so-called Ancient Mode of Production in particular, constantly evokes among Marxist and non-Marxist scholars in France and Italy (in complete contrast to West Germany and Great Britain)'.[20]

Kreissig's comment about West Germany refers primarily to the work undertaken by the Committee for Ancient History of the Academy of Sciences and Literature at Mainz, under the auspices of Joseph Vogt (1895–1986), together with Finley the other main recent influence on the study of ancient slavery.[21] Vogt's decision after the war to devote himself to organizing a programme for the study of Greek and Roman slavery in all its aspects may be seen as a kind of 'intellectual reparations' to a dispossessed and exploited class to make up for his failure, as a committed Catholic, to stand up publicly against Nazism. Unlike the British and the French, the Germans had hardly been involved in the modern slave-trade, and consequently had hitherto been less sensitive about ancient slavery. Vogt's interest in slavery was not because it was different from, but rather because he felt that it was similar to, the worst experiences of twentieth-century Europeans.

Many of the monographs produced by the Academy contain extremely detailed and scholarly analyses of particular problems, but disappointingly fail to relate these to a wider picture of ancient slavery.[22] This is less a reaction to the blatantly ideological Marxist studies on slavery produced in the German language during the Stalinist era, than a result of the career structure of German universities, in which young scholars are well advised not to write anything controversial until they hold a tenured post. Hence a series of largely empirical studies along the lines laid out by Vogt himself. Nor should Vogt's emphasis on 'Humanity' as a way of synthesizing the work of his school be seen as specifically anti-communist. In post-1945 Germany, the 'Third Humanism' was one intellectual tradition that had been resistant to Nazi ideology, and could thus be exploited by communist as well as western scholars.[23]

Some of the work produced on slavery since the war has of course been undertaken by scholars untouched by, if not oblivious to, these controversies. But it is apparent that ancient slavery is one area where scholars have to be very clear about their view of social history in general (whether they admit to an 'ideology', to using 'models', or just a 'method') before proceding to what they would be entitled to claim was an objective assessment of the evidence.

NOTES

The abbreviations *GARS* stands for *Greek and Roman Slavery* (Croom Helm, London, 1981), the present writer's selection of translated excerpts from ancient sources. The book contains a bibliography of works up to 1980, largely in English, on pp. 252–8.

1. The second edition of N. Brockmeyer, *Bibliographie zur Antiken Sklaverei* (ed. E. Herrmann, Bochum, 1983) lists 5162 books and articles, and is very far from complete. For a good bibliographical survey, see N. Brockmeyer, *Antike Sklaverei* (Darmstadt, 1979).

2. D. B. Davis, *The Problem of Slavery in Western Culture* (Cornell U.P., 1966) and *The Problem of Slavery in the Age of Revolution* (Cornell U.P., 1975); H. Craton/J. Walvin/D. Wright, *Slavery, Abolition and Emancipation* (London, 1976); J. Walvin (ed.), *Slavery and British Society 1776–1846* (Baton Rouge, 1982); C. Bolt & S. Drescher, *Anti-Slavery, Religion and Reform: Essays in Memory of Roger Anstey* (Folkestone, 1980). Benjamin Disraeli described the anti-slavery agitation as a 'humbug damnable' (1846: C. Whibley, *Lord John Manners and his Friends* (Edinburgh, 1925), I, 222). Cf. Cobbett's remarks about the hypocrisy of the pro-abolition elite in *Rural Rides* (1825).

3. M. L. Gordon, 'The Nationality of Slaves under the Early Roman Empire', *JRS* 14 (1924), 111. The traditional view of slave promiscuity was demolished by B. Rawson, 'Roman Concubinage', *TAPhA* 104 (1974), 279 ff.

4. H. W. Pleket, 'Technology in the Greco-Roman World: A General Report', *Talanta* 5 (1975), 6–47.

5. Amongst the dozens of works written from a Christian perspective, H. Wallon, *Histoire de l'esclavage dans l'antiquité*, 3 vols (Paris, 1847; 1879²; reprinted Aalen, 1974), and P. Allard, *Les esclaves chrétiens* (Paris, 1876), were particularly influential.

6. O. Patterson, *Slavery and Social Death* (Harvard U.P., 1982).

7. K. Hopkins, *Death and Renewal* (Cambridge, 1983), ch. I; J. Vogt, 'Der Sterbende Sklave: Vorbild menschlicher Vollendung' in *Sklaverei und Humanität. Ergänzungsheft* (Wiesbaden, 1983), pp. 6–16.

8. 'Marxism is not a science of history, it is a theory of contemporary politics and its use of history will always be selective by reason of its political concerns' (P. Q. Hirst, *Marxism and Historical Writing* (London, 1985), p. 146).

9. H. Heinen (ed.), *Die Geschichte des Altertums im Spiegel der sowjetischen Forschung* (Darmstadt, 1980).
The leading Soviet ancient history journal is *Vestnik Drevneii Istorii* ('Journal of Ancient History'), which first appeared in 1939. Several major Russian works on ancient slavery have been translated into German under the auspices of the Mainz Academy.
Some English Marxist views of the end of the ancient world: F. W. Walbank, *The Awful Revolution* (London, 1968²); P. Anderson, *Passages from Antiquity to Feudalism* (London, 1975); E. A. Thompson, 'Peasant Revolts in Late Roman Gaul and Spain', *Past & Present* 1 (1952), 1–23.

10. C. Mosse, *The Ancient World at Work* (Engl. transl., London, 1969); A. M. Burford, *Craftsmen in Greek and Roman Society* (London, 1972); and ch. IV p. 30 below.

11. Plato's failure to distinguish serfs from slaves: *Laws* 776b–778a (= *GARS* 80, p. 83). Tacitus on the Germans: *Germania* 24.3–25.3 (= *GARS* 20). For helots as 'slaves' in the Marxist sense, cf. P. Cartledge, *Sparta and Lakonia* (London, 1979), ch. 10, considerably qualified in P. Cartledge, 'Rebels and Sambos in Classical Greece', *CRUX* (Exeter, 1985), 40–46.

12. Solon's *seisachtheia*: O. Murray, *Early Greece* (Glasgow, 1980), ch. 11.

13. A. M. Bailey & F. R. Llobera, *The Asiatic Mode of Production* (London, 1981). The concept of an Ancient Mode of Production plays an important role in Y. Garlan, *Les Esclaves en Grèce antique* (Paris, 1982), an excellent survey from a neo-Marxist point of view; an English translation is in preparation.

14. W. L. Westermann, *The Slave Systems of Greek and Roman Antiquity* (Philadelphia, 1955), an expansion of his article on 'Sklaverei' for *RE* Suppl. VI (Stuttgart, 1935), 894–1068.

15. Two straightforward introductions to Weber's ideas are: D. G. Macrae, *Weber* (London, 1974) and F. Parkin, *Max Weber* (Chichester, 1982).

16. K. Löwith, *Max Weber and Karl Marx* (London, 1982). For Polanyi, cf. esp. K. Polanyi, *Primitive, Archaic and Modern Economies* (ed. G. Dalton, Boston, 1971).

17. M. I. Finley, *The Ancient Economy* (London, 1973); this approach had much earlier been applied to the Mycenean and Homeric worlds, cf. M. I. Finley, *Economy and Society in Ancient Greece* (ed. B. D. Shaw and R. P. Saller, London, 1981). The 'Editors' Introduction' discusses Finley's intellectual development and contribution to ancient history.

18. Cf. the conference at Rome in 1981 devoted to Finley's *Ancient Slavery and Modern Ideology* (London, 1980; French, German, and Italian translations), and published as *OPUS: International Journal for Social and Economic History of Antiquity* 1 (1982), fasc. 1., p. 3 & 81.

19. Besançon 1970–73; other *colloques sur l'esclavage* whose papers have been published include those at Nieborow, Poland, 1975; Brixen/Bressanone, 1976; and one on *Antike Abhäng-igkeitsformen* at Jena, 1981.

20. H. Kreissig, 'Zur Sklaverei im Altertum. Eine Zwischenbilanz der Internationalen Colloques sur l'esclavage', *Jahrbuch für Wirtschaftsgeschichte* 1978 (3), 126 f.

21. Some of Vogt's essays have been translated into English as *Ancient Slavery and the Ideal of Man* (Oxford/Harvard U.P., 1974).

22. The chapter on 'Ancient Slavery and Modern Ideology' in Finley's book of that title contains a systematic critique of Vogt's approach: in Finley's terms, 'antiquarian' rather than genuine 'analytic' history.

23. E. John, 'Antiker und sozialistischer Humanismus', *Klio* 57 (1975), 15–21 (title of a scientific colloquium of the Central Institute for Ancient History and Archaeology of the Academy of Sciences of the German Democratic Republic, 28–30 October 1971).

II. INTERPRETING THE EVIDENCE

Literary Texts

Attempts to find statements reflecting the attitudes and experiences of slaves have met with no more success than the search for those of women. The most likely possibilities are the fables and moral *sententiae* ascribed to known slaves or freedmen, such as Aesop and Phaedrus. But even here things are not as straightforward as they have seemed to some.[1] Fables universalize the human experience; they may use the slave situation to illustrate that experience, but it does not follow that they are expressing any real slave's point of view. In any case, the literary form of the fable makes it authoritarian – one can only accept or reject the moral of a fable, not argue rationally against it. In fact it encapsulates the advice which older adults give to children: if the genre was originally intended for children, then the reason why it was ascribed to the slave Aesop may well have been that the children of the Greek elite were brought up by slave nurses and *paedagogi* (childminders rather than 'tutors').

Certainly most of the literature which survives from classical Greek and Roman antiquity was written by adult male citizens to be recited to audiences of adult male citizens. As we have seen, slavery was crucial to the way in which the citizen community defined its position. Consequently slavery is mentioned in a vast range of texts belonging to different literary genres; and the proper interpretation of any of these passages requires an awareness of the rules applying to the relevant genre, including the types of characters, the *topoi* (commonplaces), the rhetorical arguments and the vocabulary which the audience would have expected the author to use. Members of the Greek and Roman citizen elite who wrote works of philosophy or literature were not interested in preserving 'objective' information about slavery for later historians: they were using their idea of what slavery meant in order to communicate with other citizens. They were not thinking *about* slavery so much as using the concept 'slavery' to think *with*.

Thus the frequency with which a writer refers to slaves will tell us about that writer's conceptual world, rather than the social world in which he actually lived. Since epic is intended to describe an heroic world, and slaves symbolize the extreme opposite of heroism, slaves tend not to appear in Greek or Latin epic poetry. But the almost uncanny absence of slaves from the *Aeneid* allows us to draw no conclusions about the place of slavery in Vergil's Rome. Nor does the fact that an individual slave may appear in a major literary role tell us anything about the economic importance of slavery, or about how the author treated any actual slaves he may have encountered himself. The slave swineherd Eumaeus in the *Odyssey* is an example. If we bear in mind the Structuralist notion of the slave as being at the edge of society, then it becomes clear that the poet gives him a major role because the reconstitution of proper social relationships within Odysseus' household is a central theme of the poem. Because a slave swineherd living at the edge of the community is the lowest member of the household, Odysseus on his return to Ithaca must begin by re-establishing the paternal relationship that binds him to that slave. This is a statement about how the social world ought to be, not a description of what relations between masters and slaves were actually like in Homer's time. Not that Homer is unaware of how slaves were treated in reality: 'I fear he will be angry with me, for the scoldings of masters are severe', Eumaeus says at 17.188 f.[2]

This approach to how slavery was used as a *concept* by ancient writers is an advance on more traditional literary studies whose primary purpose was to list exhaustively and to categorize types of occurrences in ancient literature, and which tended to take such references at their face value. While the slave types of Greek and Roman comedy may have had some basis in real experience,[3] they were also founded on the prejudices and expectations of the citizen audience. Slaves are lazy, sex-crazed, or gluttonous, and they are there to be beaten. The same applies to Roman satire, and to Petronius' satirical travesty of the Greek love-romance, the *Satyricon*: his slaves and freedmen are caricatures, and they cannot be turned into real life figures simply by scaling down the comic exaggeration.[4]

Numbers and statistics are a particular problem. Few would now treat Petronius' exaggerations as 'statistics', but even the figures given for prices and numbers of slaves by encyclopaedists like Pliny the Elder and Athenaeus present copious problems of interpretation. Anecdotes are not chosen for being typical, but for being impressive or even extreme. For a Roman, being accompanied by only a few slaves might either be a cause for shame, or alternatively a sign of old-fashioned virtue.[5] Athenaeus' remark that in 312/08 B.C. a census revealed that there were 21,000 citizens, 10,000 Metics and 400,000 *oiketai* at Athens is a good illustration of the problem.[6] Athenaeus lived 500 years later; his manuscript text is corrupt; we can only speculate on the context of the census (probably Demetrius of Phaleron's preparations for a siege); and we have no idea of how reliable either Athenaeus' sources, or the census itself, may have been. Most crucially, we have to decide what Athenaeus, or his sources, meant by *oiketai*. Some scholars, especially traditionalist Marxists keen to maximize the role of slavery, still think that these were chattel-slaves, and that they constituted 93% of the population.[7] *Oiketēs* certainly can refer to slaves: but the word is not identical to *doulos*. It may refer to anyone who belongs to the household (*oikos*); and in this case, it may well include the male citizens' wives, children, and free dependants, if the objective of the census was to establish how many mouths would have to be fed in the event of a siege.

The distinctions between the different words used to refer to slaves in Greek is thus more than just an academic question. German and French scholars have established that some words are typical of a particular literary genre, others occur in different contexts. Seen as war-booty or as an item of property, a slave is an *andrapodon* ('man-footed': it does not follow that the Greeks saw their slaves as analogous to four-footed beasts other than on those occasions when they were reckoning up their wealth). From the point of view of what he does, he is a *therapōn* (servant: not, we may note, a producer). As a member of the household who has claims to be fed, clothed, and protected, he is an *oiketēs*. And as someone who lacks absolutely the rights of a citizen, he is a *doulos*. One interesting question which has yet to be satisfactorily answered is just why the word *doulos* rapidly became the most important of the words used for slaves in Greek literature from about 500 B.C. on. This must be connected with the idea of the free citizen; but it is not clear just how the primacy of the slave/free polarity is linked to Solon's abolition of the intermediate status of the *hektēmoroi*, to the overthrow of tyranny, and perhaps to the Persian king's choice of the word *doulos* to describe his officials and other members of his household.[8]

The importance of the slave/free distinction in Greek political thought means that we have to be very careful about assuming that philosophers like Aristotle are being descriptive rather than using slaves as markers for one extreme of the human condition. Thus when Aristotle discusses slaves as 'instruments', he is not telling us how he and his contemporaries saw, let alone treated, their own slaves, but conceptualizing the relationship between the man who gives orders and the man who carries them out: a (free) ship's crew is equally the 'instrument' of the ship's captain.[9] On the other hand Stoic injunctions to treat slaves properly are no evidence that masters who happened to be Stoics improved the conditions of their slaves. Slaves appear because they are one extreme pole of humanity, not because Stoics wished to reform or abolish slavery.[10] A fine Stoic paradox was to talk about kingship, the other limit of human existence, as a form of slavery.[11] From the fifth century B.C. on, many of the instances when Greeks talk about *douleia* and, later, Romans of *servitus* are not about the social institution of slavery at all, but about the metaphor of political slavery: the absence of freedom. Christian writers use the words in similar ways. When St Paul proclaims the irrelevance of 'the question of Greek and Jew, circumcised and uncircumcised, barbarian, Scythian, freeman, slave: Christ is all' (Colossians 3:11), he is not abolishing social and cultural distinctions, but claiming that each group has a place within the Christian church. Paul goes on to order slaves to obey their earthly masters unconditionally (3:22–4).[12] Apologists who argue that Christianity was opposed to slavery in principle fail to recognize that Christian writers, like everyone else in antiquity, mention slaves precisely because they represent the polar opposite to the free citizen. When in Late Antiquity the free citizen ceased to be socially central, but was replaced by the Christian, then the slave, like the barbarian, became less interesting conceptually, and was replaced by other symbols of marginality such as the monk. Slavery continued to exist, and throughout the Middle Ages slaves continued to perform much the same functions in the Mediterranean area as they had in the classical period. The hypothesis of a shift from slavery to serfdom as an 'explanation' (or even 'definition') of the Middle Ages is a myth, though it may well be true that in some geographical areas, such as Norman England, 'feudalism' (in the strict sense of the word), by making everyone a dependant, made formal slavery irrelevant.[13] But this certainly did not happen in Late Antiquity: slaves did not disappear from the real world, but only from the thoughts and words of writers who viewed the world from a religious, and not a political, perspective.

Archaeology and Epigraphy

Neither vase-paintings nor sculptural monuments normally explicitly indicate the status of the individuals depicted. Before such evidence can be used to throw light on the activities of slaves, or on attitudes towards them, we first need to have criteria for identifying which figures in fact depict slaves. The fact that they are engaged in agricultural or craft work is no safe indication, since free citizens and slaves (and often owners together with their own slaves) worked side-by-side in the fields and workshops. We can be more certain that servants shown dressing their mistress's hair, massaging their master's foot, helping a drunk to get home, and fetching or carrying things, are intended to be slaves.[14] But status cannot be derived from function. Clothes worn may be an indication, although it is impossible to

1. A slave massages his master's foot.

2. A slave girl with cropped hair holds a box for her mistress.

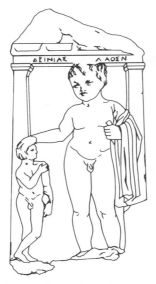

3. Tombstone of a child with his *paedagogus*.

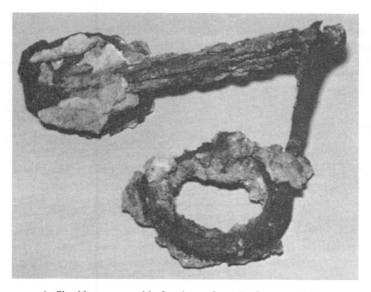

4. Shackles, presumably for slaves, from the Laureum mines.

isolate absolutely consistent conventions. Where Roman citizens are shown wearing the toga, men in short tunics may be slaves. The servant Hegeso wears the long sleeves of a barbarian on an Athenian relief of ca. 380 B.C.: is this a sign that she is a slave? Size and physiognomy are more reliable indications. Since a slave is less important than a citizen, he is often drawn much smaller: this has nothing to do with whether he is a child or not. One Athenian grave monument has a large child attended by his much smaller slave *paedagogus*. Sometimes these small slaves are fast asleep – an indication of the free world's prejudice that slaves are indolent and work-shy. The frequency of representations of blacks, particularly as entertainers, is the result of an understandable fascination with 'marginal' types: but confusion between ethnic/geographical and social marginality makes it difficult to be certain which if any of these blacks were meant to be slaves.[15]

These problems facing traditional art-history are shared by the 'New Archaeology' with its interest in the social context of buildings and artefacts. Here too it is difficult to know when material remains point to the presence of a social status rather than an industry or a service. Only a very firm believer in the Marxist correlation between social and economic phenomena will argue that particular building techniques indicate the presence of slaves.[16] It seems obvious to some that leg shackles found in the Athenian silver mines at Laureum were used to restrain slaves. But would all slaves have been treated in this way, or only those who had tried to run away, or had assaulted overseers or other workers? When such shackles date to the Roman period, they may have been intended not for slaves, but for criminals condemned to work in the mines as a punishment, whatever their status.

The use of papyrological and epigraphic evidence involves its own particular problems. Papyri are found in restricted geographical zones. While they have been used to good effect, as by Professor Biezunska-Malowist of Warsaw University, for classical Egypt,[17] the picture they present may not apply to other areas of the Mediterranean world. The archives of Jucundus from Pompeii and other papyrus documents buried by the lava of Vesuvius may give a more typical picture of economic affairs in a first-century A.D. Italian municipality.[18] Attempts to use epigraphical and papyrus evidence to compile statistics about the numbers and sex-ratios of slaves, fluctuations in their price, frequency of manumission and life-expectancy, have encountered a whole range of problems of interpretation.[19] The atypicality of the surviving evidence is itself significant: the great over-representation of freedmen in inscriptions from Rome is an interesting indication of their, and their heirs', anxiety to ensure that everyone was aware that they had achieved full integration as citizens.

Roman Law

Some of the earliest academic studies of ancient slavery, in the seventeenth and eighteenth centuries, were undertaken by lawyers interested in the problems which slavery posed to the Roman legal system. Classical scholars and ancient historians have generally been less aware of the wealth of material about slavery provided by Roman legal texts than they might have been. Partly this has been because Theodor Mommsen (1817–1904) and his followers were more interested in using the Codes to reconstruct liberty than social or economic slavery. Because Common Law reigns supreme in England (not Scotland), acquaintance with Roman law here has hitherto been relatively rare.[20]

Historians of law tend to see the object of their studies as an autonomous and coherent system; social historians on the other hand have to ask how the system related to the realities of life at the time. It is remarkable that if we compare the *Digest* with the roughly contemporary Jewish law-code, the *Mishnah*,[21] we find that although slaves and slavery were performing the same sorts of functions in both societies, they are referred to much more frequently by Roman jurists. Was this because Roman law was intended for an elite of considerably richer families, whose conflicts might involve slaves they owned or had freed, or had given or hired out to one another? Does Roman law simply ignore the peasant smallholder and the hired labourer, so frequently mentioned in the *Mishnah*, because such lowly citizens could never make use of their constitutional rights to engage in litigation against the upper orders? Or, on the contrary, does classical Roman law accurately reflect the repressive needs of the dominant class in a slave-holding society?[22]

There are more general problems of interpretation. The *Digest* was compiled in the sixth century A.D., but includes material from up to seven centuries earlier. How can we place this earlier material within the general system of legal thought of its time when we do not know its original context? To what extent has it been brought up to date? And since Justinian's Roman empire had been Christian for over two centuries, his law codes tell us next to nothing about slavery in the context of pagan religious rites and institutions.

There are further difficulties about trying to explain particular pieces of legislation in terms of a political situation or a long-term trend. Throughout the imperial period, emperors legislated to protect slaves. Were they influenced by 'humanitarian' feelings inculcated by Stoicism and, later, Christianity? Were they trying to make the slave's condition less onerous in order to avoid the complete breakdown of slavery in the face of the 'crisis of slave-holding society' caused by the hypothetical drying-up of external sources of new slaves?[23] Or were the emperors less interested in protecting slaves than in finding ever wider reasons for interfering with and controlling the lives of their masters? Perhaps one should look for specific rather than general explanations: were Claudius' interventions in favour of slaves, such as the *Senatusconsultum Claudianum* which allowed imperial slaves to marry free women, or his freeing of sick slaves abandoned by their masters, merely the result of pressure from his over-mighty freedmen-secretaries? This is an area where it is clearly dangerous to jump to conclusions. Eastern as well as western scholars are agreed that the *Digest* and the *Codes* still have a great deal to reveal on the subject of slavery.[24]

NOTES

1. J. Christes, 'Reflexe erlebter Unfreiheit in den Sentenzen des Publilius Syrus und den Fabeln des Phaedrus', *Hermes* 107 (1979), 199–220.

2. G. P. Rose, 'The Swineherd and the Beggar', *Phoenix* 34 (1980), 285–97.

3. V. Ehrenberg, *The People of Aristophanes* (Oxford, 1951); P. P. Spranger, *Historische Untersuchungen zu den Sklavenfiguren des Plautus und Terenz* (Wiesbaden, 1984²); C. Stace, 'The Slaves of Plautus', *G & R* 15 (1968), 64–77.

4. P. Veyne, 'Vie de Trimalcion', *Annales E.S.C.* 166 (1961), 213–47.

5. Apuleius, *Apol.* 17 (= *GARS* 81).

6. Athenaeus, *Deipn.* 272 c (= *GARS* 80 p. 90).

7. L. Canfora in *OPUS* (ch. I n. 18 above), pp. 33–48.

8. F. Gschnitzer, *Studien zur griechischen Terminologie der Sklaverei* I (Wiesbaden, 1964) and II (Wiesbaden, 1976); M.-M. Mactoux *Douleia. Esclavage et Pratiques Discursives dans l'Athènes Classique* (Paris, 1980).

9. Aristotle, *Pol.* 1, 2.4 (= *GARS* 2 p. 17). Cf. the use of the word *instrumentum* in Latin, or phrases like 'natural wastage' in English.

10. M. T. Griffin, 'Seneca on Slavery', *Seneca: A Philosopher in Politics* (Oxford, 1976), pp. 256–85 & 458–61; P. A. Brunt, 'Aspects of the Social Thought of Dio Chrysostom and of the Stoics', *PCPhS* 199 (1973), 9–34.

11. H. Volkmann, 'Die basileia als *endoxos douleia*', *Historia* 16 (1967), 155–61.

12. S. S. Bartchy, *First Century Slavery and the Interpretation of I Corinthians 7 : 21* (Missoula, Montana, 1973); F. Laub, *Die Begegnung des frühen Christentums mit der Sklaverei* (Stuttgart, 1982).

13. That the idea that slavery disappeared in the early Middle Ages was untenable was already seen by M. Bloch, 'Comment et pourquoi finit l'esclavage antique?', *Annales E.S.C.* 2 (1947), 30–44 and 161–70; reprinted in M. I. Finley (ed.), *Slavery in Classical Antiquity* (Cambridge, 1968²), 204–28. Cf. C. Verlinden, *L'Esclavage dans l'Europe Médiévale* (Gent, 1977); P. Dockès, *Medieval Slavery and Liberation* (Engl. trans., Methuen, 1982); W. D. Phillips, Jr., *Slavery from Roman Times to the Early Transatlantic Trade* (Minnesota/Manchester, 1985).

14. The most accessible short survey I know of is N. Himmelmann, *Archäologisches zum Problem der griechischen Sklaverei* (Wiesbaden, 1971).

15. J. Vercoutter (ed.), *The Image of the Black in Western Art* I (New York, 1976); F. M. Snowden, *Blacks in Antiquity* (Harvard U.P., 1970) and *Before Color Prejudice* (Harvard U.P., 1983).

16. 'Opus reticulatum – technique de construction caracteristique de l'exploitation esclavagiste': *Esclaves et Maitres en Etrurie Romaine* (1981 French translation of the exhibition catalogue *Schiavi e Padroni* of 1979), p. 56.

17. I. Biezunska-Malowist, *L'esclavage dans l'Egypte greco-romaine* I (Warsaw, 1974); II (1977), together with over thirty individual articles.

18. J. Andreau, *Les Affaires de Monsieur Jucundus* (Rome, 1974).

19. J. Harper, 'Slaves and Freedmen in Imperial Rome', *AJPh* 93 (1972), 341ff.; M. Clauss, 'Probleme der Lebensalterstatistiken aufgrund römischer Grabinschriften', *Chiron* 3 (1973), 395–427.

20. The standard English textbook remains W. W. Buckland, *The Roman Law of Slavery* (Cambridge, 1908).

21. There is a useful English translation by H. Danby (Oxford, 1933). Cf. M. Goodman, *State and Society in Roman Galilee A.D. 132–212* (Totowa, 1983).

22. G. Härtel, 'Einige Bemerkungen zur rechtlichen Stellung der Sklaven im 2/3 Jht. u.Z. anhand der Digesten', *Klio* 59 (1977), 337–47, a traditional Marxist discussion.

23. H. Langenfeld, *Christianisierungspolitik und Sklavengesetzgebung der römischen Kaiser* (Bonn, 1977); E. M. Staerman, 'Die ideologische Vorbereitung des Zusammenbruchs der Produktionsweise der Sklavereigesellschaft', *Klio* 60 (1978), 225–33, by a leading Soviet scholar, argues that Stoicism and Christianity, by 'humanizing' the practice of slavery, were trying to overcome the crisis of slaveholding society caused by the drying-up of sources of new captives.

24. M. Morabito, *Les Realités de l'esclavage d'après le Digeste* (Paris, 1981), fails to live up to its promising title.

III. SLAVERY AS A SOCIAL INSTITUTION

Whatever our view of the compatibility of Marx's theories with Weber's, ancient slavery can be better understood if it is approached primarily as a social category rather than as an economic class. It is the slave's total rightlessness against his master which makes slavery a 'peculiar institution' compared with other forms of dependence. The slave was someone who had lost, or never had, any rights to share in society, and therefore to have access to food, clothing, and the other necessities of physical survival. Typically this was because a slave had been on the defeated side in a war. Roman jurists derived the word *servus* from *servatus*.[1] The victors could have killed him: he had no moral claims on them to allow him the means to survive. But the victors had chosen to let him live. Consequently the enslaved captive 'belonged' to the individual who had refrained from killing him, or to his community, which generally sold him off to an individual. The fact that he was alive at all was something that the slave owed to his captor, and the fact that he was subsequently kept alive was something he owed to the master who deigned to maintain him as a member of his household. The emotions he was expected to feel towards that master were loyalty and gratitude.[2] Any children the slave might have would inherit this dependence: they would only be alive at all because the head of the household chose to bring them up, feed, clothe, house, and train them, rather than let them die (of course he had a similar right to let his own new-born children live or die).[3]

Wars are spectacular occasions prominent in ancient literature, and probably considerably over-emphasized as sources of slavery by ancient writers as well as modern historians (particularly those Marxists who see ancient imperialism primarily as a mechanism for obtaining additional labour in the form of slaves). Greek and Roman masters liked to think that they were justified in owning the slaves who served them, e.g. because they had been born and brought up on their estates or had been captured in a just war. Our sources under-emphasize two of the major and constant sources of new slaves in the ancient world, kidnapping and piracy in time of 'peace', and the enslaving of new-born children exposed by their parents, or of not-so-new-born children sold by them to slave-traders. Roman law did not recognize that a free-born person could become a slave in this way. Those Greeks who thought about the issue were equally sceptical about whether such unfortunates truly became slaves.

The lack of interest in the mechanisms of the slave trade by ancient writers is peculiar, and suggests that they had an uneasy conscience about the extent to which their slaves did not in fact 'deserve' that status. The ideal was for one's slaves to have been born into the household (*oikogeneis, vernae*). This was not a response to any difficulties in obtaining war-captives, but a constant moral attitude. It masked the moral doubts aroused by the slave trade, and made it unnecessary for a master to worry about whether the people who served him had been justly enslaved.[4]

If the slave ideally owed his entire existence to the master who was 'saving' him from death and starvation, then this explains why the slave had no right even to his own name. There have been many studies of the names of Greek and Roman slaves since the beginning of this century; early assumptions that these names necessarily indicated ethnic or geographical origin have now been abandoned. Some of the names which masters gave their slaves were associated with particular ethnic groups (e.g. Geta, Daos, Syrus), but most were not. Masters were as likely to wish to associate their slaves with a god (Hermes, Dionysus), or assert their wealth and status by calling their slaves by a name reminiscent of luxury (Tryphon, Felix).[5]

The absoluteness of a master's rights included the right to punish his slave without having to fear any outside legal constraint; after all, the slave's life was a gift from the master. Where there were constraints, they were not intended to protect the slave against the master, but the state or community at large against a master whose power might threaten other citizens. Thus Athenian law allowed any citizen to prosecute a master who behaved tyrannically towards his slaves for *hybris*, the arrogance ascribed to tyrants.[6] But slaves themselves had no legal rights; where Greek writers condemn the murder of slaves, it is on general moral grounds, or in order to buttress a specific rhetorical argument such as the superiority of Athens to Sparta.[7] Those who harmed slaves in any way had to pay for the damage they caused – but the damage was to the master's rights in the slave, not to the slave, whose inferior status was made manifest by the fact that the fine was much smaller than that imposed for harming a free man.[8] Legally, slaves had no personality; since the faculty of free choice was denied them (having no will independent of their master's), it was accepted in Greece as in Rome that slaves could only be assumed to tell the truth in a court of law if their testimony had been given under torture.[9] Roman law allowed limited exceptions to the principle that no slave could lay information against the master from who he derived his being: in the republic, *vis publica* (including rebellion and riot) and *incestum*, ritual offences against purity which offended the gods, most spectacularly sexual irregularities by Vestal Virgins. From the time of Augustus on, there was a radical change in state interference in a master's rights over his slaves, in particular through the *Lex Julia de adulteriis coercendis*, the legislation of 18 B.C. making adultery a criminal offence and transferring its punishment from the domestic jurisdiction of the *paterfamilias* and his *consilium* to that of a state court. In adultery cases, slaves could now inform against their own masters, as they could in cases of treason (*maiestas*). Some attempt was made to preserve the fiction that an owner's rights were absolute. Augustus arranged for slaves to be bought either by himself or by the state before accepting their testimony against their masters. But in general such restrictions on the rights of owners are a sign of the transfer of power from the citizen-community to the emperor, not of any improvement in the conditions of slaves.[10]

Restrictions on a master's right to punish his slaves as he pleased should be seen as part of the same tendency for the emperor to extend his control over private citizens, rather than as evidence of 'humanitarianism' or as a response to alleged difficulties in finding new sources of slave labour from beyond the frontiers of the empire. When the *Lex Petronia* (late 1st c. A.D.) forbade owners from selling their slaves to fight beasts in the arena, it forced them to go before a public court if they wanted to execute disobedient slaves; it did not stop slaves from being punished in this particular way. An inscription from Puteoli illustrates the typically Roman concern for detail in regulations about how public contractors were to go about crucifying condemned slaves.[11] There was no intention to protect slaves, but to subject their owners to control; and Roman jurists found it difficult to reconcile such control with the theory that a master's power was absolute.[12]

The absence of legal restrictions meant that only moral sentiment or self-interest prevented a master from behaving callously or sadistically towards his slave. Ancient writers report many anecdotes about the inhumanity of masters: how Vedius Pollio ordered a boy who had broken a valuable crystal cup to be executed by being thrown to the beasts, in this case some lampreys he kept in his fishpond, or how the emperor Hadrian lost his temper with a secretary and poked out his eye with a pen.[13] Such atrocities were invariably reported in order to be condemned. So was Cato's recommendation that old or sick slaves should be sold. It is controversial what the point exactly was that Cato wished to make, but it was accepted that an owner had a moral obligation to look after any slaves who were sick or too old to work. Claudius ordered sick slaves abandoned by their owners to be freed (with entitlement to the state corn dole?). The evidence for what happened to slaves who survived to an age where they could no longer work is sparse, and not yet systematically collated. No doubt reality fell far short of any ideal, as in our own society.[14]

If such harshness was condemned, beating was not. On the contrary, as in other slave-owning cultures, physical violence by master against slave was regarded as right and proper. The philosopher Ammonius once felt that his students had had too much for lunch; he had a slave beaten during the afternoon lecture in order to provide them with a warning on the necessity for self-control.[15] Such an attitude is so difficult for twentieth-century Europeans to understand that some have seen it as part of a conscious attempt to terrorize slaves, on the assumption that only systematic terror could stop them from throwing off their chains and ending the slave system.[16] Perhaps a better explanation can be found in the conceptual inferiority of slaves: like children or barbarians, slaves are outside the fully human citizen community. While communication with fellow-citizens takes place through the medium of rational discourse (Gk. *logos*), slaves are subjected to beatings to show that they do not belong to that community. The ancient world tolerated violence to a degree which most modern Europeans find quite unacceptable; but beating is not random terror. It establishes a social hierarchy: of husband over wife, parents (or teachers) over children, freepersons over slaves. Slaves themselves were human enough to beat animals.

From the standpoint of the adult male citizen, women, children, and barbarians are all 'marginal'. This raises the question of whether there were analogies between their treatment and that of slaves. In both Greece and Rome, slaves were seen as similar to children; they were addressed as children (Gk. vocative *pai*, Lat. *puer*). Unlike free children, they had no right to expect that they would ever 'come of age'. It may be worth bearing in mind that, given the low life-expectancy, a large proportion of slaves (as of the population at large) actually were children.

Ancient literature ascribes to slaves an assortment of vices and shortcomings which are not unlike those ascribed to women.[17] They are lazy, talkative, interested only in food, sex, and sleep, compulsive liars, and steal the wine. These are crude prejudices, but the evidence shows that they were constants, at least from Aristophanes' time to that of late antique Christian writers like Salvian.

The identification of slaves and barbarians by some Greek thinkers was more serious, both intellectually and because of its effect on early modern attitudes towards negro slavery. Isocrates and others in the fourth century B.C. had anchored their belief in the cultural superiority of Greeks over others in the use of a shared language, and went on to identify the *logos* of rhetoric with the *logos* of reason. From there it was a short step for Aristotle to deduce that barbarians were natural slaves, needing masters to help them through life with the *logos* which only Greeks possessed. This was essentially a cultural, not a racial, prejudice (any barbarian who learnt Greek participated in *logos*); but it has never been easy to distinguish culture from racial origin. In Aristophanes, slaves are pilloried for their bad Greek, and Athenian pottery depicting negroes and Scythians suggests that the peoples who inhabited the fringes of the world were perceived as grotesque and naturally inferior, rather than simply different. As marginal figures, blacks reinforced the marginality of slaves – for Theophrastus' 'prestige-seeking man', as for early modern European aristocrats, it was especially classy to be served by a slave who was black.[18]

Roman prejudice also identified particular races as servile, but was not so systematic.[19] This was partly because Romans traditionally had no qualms about enslaving Italians from other states, while many Greeks as early as the fifth century B.C. felt that Greek-speakers ought not to be permanently enslaved by fellow Greeks; and also because Rome's liberality in awarding citizenship to non-Latins and to ex-slaves meant that the Romans could not avoid being conscious that theirs was a racially mixed citizen body. Stoic cosmopolitanism may have reflected this Roman attitude, but in fact the Stoics shared the prejudice that barbarians should be enslaved to those more rational than themselves.

Our examination of slavery as a form of social dependence has stressed the brutality and degradation which resulted from the slave's lack of any independent social identity. The moral indignation which we are bound to feel at this should not be allowed to obscure the fact that slavery had some advantages for those who were enslaved. In the circumstances of the ancient world, many individuals were only alive at all because those who had destroyed their communities in warfare had had the option of enslaving instead of indiscriminately killing their enemies.[20] And many who had been exposed by their parents at birth owed their lives to the fact that slavery gave someone an incentive to feed, house, and clothe them as their slaves. Culturally and emotionally too, slavery provided a framework within which individuals who had been violently uprooted from their background – and whose social as well as material 'homes' had often been irrevocably destroyed in war – could find a new home and a new identity. At Rome, slaves and freedmen belonging to the same household frequently provided each other with the emotional support which we associate with the family unit.[21] Of course slavery was also a source of psychological insecurity: every slave will have been aware that his owner was legally entitled to beat him, even execute him, and perhaps even more terrifyingly, sell him away from the household so as to part him for ever from his loved ones. We do not have to believe that owners frequently executed or sold their slaves, or did so out of spite: the fact that it was allowed at all will have been a powerful enough incentive for slaves to repress their feelings and act to please their masters, except under the severest provocation. But while the fear of execution or sale was real, it should be considered in the context of other fears very real in ancient society. Free citizens too might be separated from their loved ones for months or (at Rome) years, by conscription for military service. Premature death from illness was an immediate reality which terrified everyone whatever their status. Membership of a (relatively) wealthy household at least gave slaves more security from starvation and hunger than many free cultivators were ever able to look forward to: what will have been terrible was being the slave of a poor man. It should not surprise us that individuals sometimes sold themselves (and not just their wives and children) into slavery. The most balanced account of the positive as well as the negative features of slavery in these terms is perhaps that by Hermann Strasburger (1909–85).[22] As one who had suffered from Nazi racism because of his Jewish descent, Strasburger was well aware that an institution which allowed outsiders a secure place within the community was preferable to physical extinction.

The logical implication of the model of slavery as an institution which gives rightless outsiders a place in society is that the outsider can be fully integrated by being freed as an equal member of the group. Manumission has been a hope held out to slaves, and an ideal believed in by their masters, in many societies.[23] Sociologists have classified slavery in different cultures as either 'closed' or 'open'.[24] It is tempting to see Greece as an instance of the former, and Rome of the latter. In Rome freed slaves were given citizenship to enable them and their descendants to be conscripted into the army and to vote for their patrons at election-time. Seen in these terms, slavery as practised at Rome would have been less a permanent status to which an individual was assigned for life, than a temporary phase which outsiders went through before joining citizen society. The proposition that a slave who survived to the age of thirty could expect to be manumitted almost as a matter of course was advocated by Geza Alföldy.[25] Unfortunately, it is based on statistical evidence which may be highly atypical, and literary testimony which requires to be taken in its proper context. Even in the imperial household (see p. 36 below), slaves were not automatically manumitted at the age of thirty: this was reserved to those required to perform managerial roles for which citizen-status was necessary. Evidence from both literature and the Roman jurists suggests that slaves were in practice freed less frequently, and after a longer period of service, than Romans liked to believe.[26] Nevertheless that belief was itself a 'fact', which will have made it easier both for masters and for slaves to come to terms with any unease they felt about their relationship.

The origins of the Roman practice of enfranchising slaves when they were freed has not yet been fully explained.[27] It cannot be isolated from Rome's willingness to share citizen-rights first with other Latin communities, and later with entirely different peoples who had proved their loyalty to Rome. That the Roman attitude was peculiar was recognized in antiquity.[28] Augustus' new regulations on the age and number of slaves who might be freed as citizens used to be seen in racial or national terms as an attempt to stem the flow of aliens from the Orontes into the Tiber. Recent interpretations have shown that Augustus was not so much interested in restricting the freeing of slaves, as in ensuring that those freed slaves who were enfranchised as full citizens (rather than 'Junian Latins') were mature and loyal, and had been fully Romanized. It was an 'acculturative programme of incentives, rewards and penalties'.[29]

The evidence concerning the frequency of manumission in Rome compared with the Greek world is insufficient to entitle us to deduce any structural differences. There is much evidence, especially epigraphic, for the freeing of slaves in many Greek states.[30] As in Rome, most of them appear to have been domestic rather than agricultural slaves, since personal service gave them access to their masters' feelings. And as in the Roman world, most freed slaves were obliged to provide their erstwhile masters with a range of services which had the effect of making the freedman's status one of dependence just as tight, if not as exacting, as that of the slave. The obligations laid upon slaves in *paramonē* ('staying') agreements might include not just a stipulated number of years' further service to the patron or his heirs, but even the provision of a child of her own to serve in the freed slave's stead. It was usual to require a money-payment to cover the cost of buying a replacement. At Rome, a freedman who became a citizen had a range of moral as well as economic obligations to his former owner (*obsequium* as well as *operae*).[31]

NOTES

1. *Digest* 1.5.2 (= *GARS* 1).
2. J. Vogt, 'The Faithful Slave', *Ancient Slavery*, pp. 129–46.
3. I know of no full-length study of exposition and infanticide in the classical world. See K. Hopkins, *Death and Renewal* (Cambridge, 1983), pp. 225f.
4. W. V. Harris, 'Towards a Study of the Roman Slave Trade', *MAAR*, 36 (1980), 117–40.
5. O. Masson, 'Les noms des esclaves dans la Grèce antique', *Actes du colloque 1971*, 9–23; H. Solin, *Beiträge zur Kenntnis der griechischen Personennamen in Rom* (Comm. human. Litt. 48, Helsinki, 1971); H. G. Pflaum, 'Sur les noms grecs portés par les Romains et leurs esclaves', *REL* 51 (1973), 48–54.
6. Dem. 21.47 (= *GARS* 183); A. R. W. Harrison, *The Law of Athens* I (Oxford, 1968), ch. 6.
7. Antiphon, *Death of Herodes* 47f. (= *GARS* 181); Isocrates, *Pan.* 181 (= *GARS* 182).
8. E.g. in the Gortyn Code (*GARS* 3), or at Rome in the Twelve Tables (*GARS* 188).
9. For Greece, e.g. Lysias 4.12ff. (= *GARS* 177); for Rome, cf. P. Brunt, 'Evidence given under Torture in the Principate', *Savigny-Zeitschrift, röm. Abt.* 97 (1980), 256–65.
10. D. Liebs, *Bollettino dell'Istituto di Diritto Romano* III 22 (1980/82), 147–89; L. Schumacher, *Servus Index. Sklavenverhör und Sklavenanzeige im republikanischen und kaiserzeitlichen Rom* (Wiesbaden, 1982).
11. *AE* 1971, No. 88.
12. Cf. Justinian, *Inst.* 1.8.2, quoting a rescript of Antoninus Pius (= *GARS* 226).
13. Vedius Pollio: Seneca, *Dial.* 5, *De Ira* 3.40 (= *GARS* 190); Dio Cassius 54, 23.1ff. Hadrian: Galen, *Diseases of the Mind* 4 (Kühn 5117) (= *GARS* 198).
14. A. E. Astin, *Cato the Censor* (Oxford, 1978), App. 12. Claudius: *Digest* 40.8.2; Suet., *Claud.* 25.2; Dio 60(61), 29.7 (= *GARS* 203 & 204). Pliny, *Ep.* 6.3, provided for one of his nurses in her old age (= *GARS* 136). Cf. A. Chantraine, ch. V n.9 below.
15. Plutarch, *Moralia* 70 E.
16. As argued by K. R. Bradley, *Slaves and Masters in the Roman Empire. A Study in Social Control* (Brussels, 1984).
17. R. Just, 'Freedom, Slavery and the Female Psyche', *CRUX* (Exeter, 1985), 169–88.
18. Theophr., *Char.* 21, the *mikrophilotimos*. For blacks in the ancient world, ch. II n. 15 above.
19. A. N. Sherwin-White, *Racial Prejudice in Imperial Rome* (Cambridge, 1967).
20. H. Volkmann, *Die Massenversklavungen der Einwohner eroberter Städte in der hellenistisch-römischen Zeit* (Wiesbaden, 1961).
21. M. B. Flory, *Family and Familia* (Yale Diss., 1975), and id., 'Family in Familia', *Am. Journal of Anc. Hist.* 3 (1978), 78–95; B. Rawson, *The Family in Ancient Rome* (London, 1986), ch. 7.
22. H. Strasburger, *Zum antiken Gesellschaftsideal* (Heidelberg, 1976).
23. For parallels in other societies, cf. Patterson, op. cit. (ch. I, n. 6), chs. 8–10. On service as a temporary phase between childhood and marriage, cf. A. Kussmaul, *Servants in Husbandry in Early Modern England* (Cambridge, 1981).
24. J. Goody, 'Slavery in Time and Space', in J. L. Watson (ed.), *Asian and African Systems of Slavery* (Oxford, 1980), pp. 16–42.
25. G. Alföldy, 'Die Freilassung von Sklaven und die Struktur der Sklaverei in der römischen Kaiserzeit', *Rivista Storica dell'Antichità* 2 (1972), 97–129 = *Die römische Gesellschaft* (Stuttgart, 1986), 286–331 (with additional discussion).
26. T. E. J. Wiedemann, 'The Regularity of Manumission at Rome', *CQ* 35 (1985), 162–75.
27. H. Chantraine, 'Zur Entstehung der Freilassung mit Bürgerrechtserwerb in Rom', *ANRW* I.2 (1972), 59–67.
28. Dio. Hal. 4.24 (= *GARS* 69).
29. K. R. Bradley, *Slaves and Masters*, p. 95; see his discussion in ch. III and Appendix D. The ultimate integration of ex-slaves is illustrated by the rise of their sons to high office: e.g. the brutal senator Larcius Macedo (Pliny, *Ep.* 3.14 = *GARS* 209). Cf. M. L. Gordon, 'The Freedman's Son in Municipal Life', *JRS* 21 (1931), 65–77.
30. K. Hopkins, *Conquerors and Slaves*, ch. 3; A. Calderini, *La Manomissione e la condizione dei liberti in Grecia* (Milan, 1980).
31. A. M. Duff, *Freedmen in the Early Empire* (Oxford, 1928; repr. 1958); S. Treggiari, *Roman Freedmen during the Late Republic* (Oxford, 1969); J. Fabre, *Libertus* (Rome, 1981).

IV. SLAVES AS PRODUCERS AND SERVANTS

To see slavery primarily as a social institution does not imply that no important economic consequences flowed from it. Slavery extends the slave-owner's capacity to do by means of his slave anything that he chooses to do; depending on the values and priorities of owners, slaves may be made to perform all sorts of functions, including economic ones, but it is only where the profit motive takes precedence over all other values, as in Western capitalism, that slaves will be treated primarily as a 'working class'. Much of the scholarship concerning itself with Greek and Roman slavery has assumed that the primary function of the institution was economic, a means of providing cheap labour as in Brazil, the Caribbean, and the southern United States. But the economic role of slaves in the ancient world should be seen in the context of the history of the ancient economy in general.[1] While slavery was not the 'cause' of any distinctive developments, it made it possible for slave-owners to react much more quickly to changes in the economy than they would have been able to if they had had to rely on autonomous or 'free' labour which would have had to be persuaded of the need for any changes.

Scholarship on the economic history of the ancient Mediterranean can, broadly speaking, be divided into two groups. The 'modernizers' have tended to emphasize technological developments which led to advances in the efficiency of agricultural or industrial production, and to stress the role of entrepreneurial commercial and trading activity in distributing such products. In its extreme (and no longer tenable) form, this approach led to the view that there had been some sort of 'industrial revolution' in Corinth and other Greek cities in the seventh/sixth centuries B.C., borne by a democratically or liberally-minded middle class of which the Athenian Metics were an important constituent. The existence of slavery was one important factor which was thought to have facilitated this qualitative advance: slaves provided the additional labour required by new industries such as vase production. Similarly, the spread of Roman imperial power in the second century B.C. was thought to have enabled Roman 'capitalists' (bankers, traders, or industrialists) to expand their commercial activities throughout the Mediterranean. Here too the existence of slavery enabled this hypothetical middle class (often identified with the equestrian *ordo* and including a significant freedman element) to make the most of its new opportunities by importing slaves in enormous numbers, primarily as producers in those agricultural and industrial sectors which were rapidly expanding (e.g. Italian wine and the

amphorae in which it was exported), and also as the shippers and
commercial agents required for distribution. Marxist scholars
argued that the republican wars of expansion were in fact fought in
order to obtain a supply of slave labour in the form of war-
captives.

The 'archaizers' on the other hand have minimized the relative
importance of trade and industry, particularly where these are
ascribed to private enterprise or to anything like the commercial
bourgeoisie which developed in European cities in the Middle Ages.
In terms of proportion (and indeed of absolute numbers), few persons
even in classical Greece and Italy won their livelihood exclusively
from commerce or industry. Wealth came overwhelmingly from agriculture, and its redistribution from primary producer to consumer took
place largely within the household unit, the *oikos* or *domus*. In the
view of the 'archaizers', it was only under quite exceptional circumstances that an agricultural unit was organized with a view to selling
its products on an open market, rather than for consumption by the
owner and his dependants (who might well, of course, be living far
away from the actual farm, typically in a political centre such as
Rome). Thus the Italian *latifundia* of the late Republic and early
empire should not be seen as similar to the large-scale sugar and cotton
plantations of the New World, worked by slave-labour because it was
cheap, and producing for a world market.[2] The ancient world did not
have the technology to create the economies of scale which make large-
scale production or processing profitable in the modern world. The
word *latifundium* does not describe a distinctive (slave) method of
production, but a form of ownership: a collection of individual units
of production, usually but not necessarily adjacent, belonging to the
same *dominus* and hence producing for the benefit of one *domus*. The
use of slaves did not necessitate or imply any qualitative changes in
the organization of the economy; it did allow vast increases in the size
of Roman households. An Italian peasant farmer could work only a
few hectares with his wife and children; in 8 B.C., the freedman
Caius Caecilius Isidorus, heir to the republican Metelli, could plough
his *latifundia* with 3,600 pair of oxen because he owned 4,116 slaves
(*GARS* 92). But the *quantitative* difference which slavery made possible was not necessarily a *qualitative* one.

The archaizers' emphasis upon the household as the fundamental
unit of production and consumption is a salutary corrective to
attempts to apply anachronistic modern conceptions of the ration-
ality of free market economics to antiquity. But it has its limitations.
While self-sufficiency was an ideal, few ancient households will ever
have achieved it. Most were too small to produce all the equipment

they required; surpluses had to be produced to reward or pay for services or goods produced by outside craftsmen, or to placate superiors by means of gifts, rent, or taxes. Even the largest *domus* was not self-sufficient. Caecilius Isidorus' 4,116 slaves could not possibly have worked all his land without the help of additional free tenants and wage labourers hired by the day. Recent research has questioned the picture of Italian agriculture in the late republic and early empire as dependent almost entirely on slaves. Peasant small-holders survived: the elite needed a large pool of free workers who could be called upon at harvest time. These free workers have left few traces in Roman legal sources because the inequality in status between them and their employers was so great that few disputes in which they were involved would ever be resolved at the formal level of a lawsuit.[3]

While seasonal labour was required primarily in arable farming, work of some kind had to be done all the year round in viticulture and herding. Both these types of agriculture were closely associated with slave labour, even though vines demand a highly-skilled work-force, and pasturage involves enormous problems regarding super-vision (described not only by the agricultural writers but also by the historians of the Sicilian and Italian slave rebellions).[4]

Although ancient economics cannot be understood without the model of the household unit, it should not lead us to ignore the circum-stances where landowners chose to maximize their revenue by pro-ducing for a market. From the second century B.C. on, the growth of Rome as an urban centre, and the existence of large Roman armies stationed overseas for long periods of time, created markets in pro-ducts such as wine, leather, and wool which Roman landowners were quick to exploit. Similar developments might have occurred even if the Romans had not had large numbers of slaves available to them at that time as a result of their wars of conquest. Other societies have produced goods for the market through peasant co-operatives or by concentrating production in factories. But as a result of their success in war, wealthy Romans found themselves with unprecedented numbers of slaves under their control; slavery enabled them to switch the productive capacity of their estates from products primarily for household consumption to products intended to be marketed. The villa at Settefinestre near Cosa in Tuscany, carefully excavated by British and Italian archaeologists from 1976 on, has been acclaimed as an illustration of this process. The evidence suggests that the estate was owned by a family called the Sestii, mentioned by Cicero; and that they used the villa to raise pigs (for ham, the staple form of preserved meat) and to produce wine, bottled in estate-produced amphorae and then exported, especially to southern and central Gaul.[5]

The development of market-directed production in the late republic cannot be explained simply as a result of a 'slave society'. But the Settefinestre discoveries certainly show that the Roman world was economically much more complex than the simple 'archaizing' interpretation would suggest. In the non-agricultural field, the model of slaves as providers of goods and services directly for their own master within the household unit needs even greater qualification. Recent work on American urban slavery has shown that many American slaves worked in the cities as craftsmen leased out by their masters, living and working on their own and paying their owners a money rent out of the wages and fees they earned, normally at equivalent rates to those earned by free black or white workers.[6] Things appear to have been similar in classical Greece and Rome, at least in some crafts and services. Sufficient epigraphical evidence survives about payments for the construction of public buildings at Athens to make it clear that free and slave craftsmen worked side-by-side, and were paid a wage in money; the slaves would be obliged to pass on part of that wage to their masters, though they might not actually be living in the *oikos* at all.[7] For other crafts, the evidence is less clear. There have been surveys of particular industries such as leather- and wool-working, baking, and especially the pottery industry (bricks, lamps, the Arretine terra-sigillata workshops),[8] but a great deal still has to be done to evaluate this information before a complete picture can emerge of the status of craftsmen in different skills, and the particular ways in which slaves were employed in them.

What is true of productive skills is equally true of services. Considerable work has gone into compiling references to slaves and freedmen performing particular services – as nurses, childminders, physicians, teachers, memory-banks, and catamites;[9] not yet, to the best of my knowledge, as doorkeepers, barbers and hairdressers, cleaners and refuse-collectors, or litter-bearers. What has not emerged is a clear picture of the circumstances under which slaves served their own masters, and how frequently they worked for someone else; and what the different juridical, social, and economic relationships might be between the owner and the employer of the slave in the particular instance.

Once slaves had been freed, their ex-masters had increased opportunities to use them in responsible positions, especially in the Roman world if they obtained full citizen rights. Freedmen could thus be used in managerial and business activity which a sufficiently wealthy master would avoid as unpleasant, onerous, or risky. The frequency with which they are depicted in literature and in epigra-

5. Slaves as workers: the exploitation of agricultural slaves in the Roman empire, as depicted in a Soviet school textbook.

6. Slaves as servants: a Roman lady having her hair dressed.

7. A Roman manumission ceremony.

8. The crucifixion of Spartacus (p. 47).

phical testimony as involved in commerce – especially high-risk activities such as banking or maritime trade – has encouraged the image of freedmen as a commercially minded 'middle class' dedicated to the rational pursuit of wealth, unlike their freeborn patrons who preferred to luxuriate on their country estates instead of maximizing profits. While it is now recognized that ancient, as well as modern, landowning aristocracies were very much concerned with the rational maximization of profits, it still seems that they preferred to leave high-risk ventures to others. Those who were successful will have been only a tiny proportion of all Greek or Roman freedmen, though their desire to prove that they had been successful through the construction of ostentatious tombs means that they are greatly over-represented in the epigraphical evidence. Whether the character of the over-ostentatious freedman as it appears in literature – Petronius' Trimalchio is the most celebrated example – is in any way a typical description of the freedman mentality seems to me to be a matter of literary criticism rather than of economic history. In any case Trimalchio, like some historical freedmen attested in literature or epigraphically, did not allow his entrepreneurial mentality to prevent him from switching his activities to the relatively risk-free and high-status ownership of land: we may assume that most wealthy freedmen similarly shared the 'mentality' of the freeborn.[10]

Some attention has been directed to the question of how slaves and freedmen got their skills in the first place.[11] Perhaps the most interesting case is that of slaves trained to be expert in Greek literature. Until recently it was supposed that the enslaving of educated Greeks from the Eastern Mediterranean and their sale to wealthy Romans was an important element in the spread of Greek culture among the Roman elite; this fitted in with some Roman fulminations against Greek culture as alien and servile. We now know that a high proportion of the slaves who taught the Romans Greek literature were not from the Greek east at all, but had been born as *vernae* in Italy or enslaved as children and chosen by their masters to be trained in the skill of Greek literature, just as others would be trained as accountants, cooks, or hairdressers.[12] Interest in Greek culture was not imported to Rome by captive slaves: slaves were educated in Greek culture because it had become fashionable for the Roman elite to display a conspicuous interest in that culture. An extreme illustration is the story of Calvisius Sabinus, who had a gang of his slaves memorize Homer, Hesiod, and the Greek lyric poets.[13] Calvisius had his slaves trained by an expert outside his own household; there are other indications that masters sent their slaves to learn *artes serviles*, such as reading, writing, and counting, at public schools.[14]

The use of slaves in mining involves separate issues and (since underground activity is uncanny, then as now) peculiar emotions. There has been detailed study of archaeological and literary evidence relating to the Athenian silver-mines at Laureum and of Roman mining activities, especially in Spain and Dacia.[15] As with other industries and services, it has become clear that it is impossible to make general statements to the effect that mining was 'normally' carried out by slaves; the regulations governing mining at Vipasca in Spain in the Flavian period show that a considerable proportion of the workers involved were free, and it is difficult to argue that they were all employed in a managerial capacity.[16] One distinction which has to be made is that between slaves who worked as miners, and *servi poenae*, convicted criminals (who might or might not be of slave status) who had been sentenced by a Roman court to work in the mines, normally but not invariably for life. The impression is that under the Empire, Rome's mines (now state owned) came to depend increasingly on this form of labour: unfree, but not chattel-slaves.[17]

NOTES

1. Two interesting analyses: M. I. Finley, *The Ancient Economy*; K. Hopkins, *Conquerors and Slaves*. Cf. also P. Garnsey, K. Hopkins & C. R. Whittaker (eds.), *Trade in the Ancient Economy* (London, 1983).

2. For the traditional view, cf. W. E. Heitland, *Agricola* (Cambridge, 1921), pp. 203–12.

3. P. Garnsey & C. R. Whittaker (eds.), *Non-Slave Labour in Greco-Roman Antiquity* (Cambridge, 1980).

4. Herdsmen in particular were at the 'margins' of city-centred social life in antiquity, and thus characteristically slaves (e.g. Eumaeus, p. 12 above). Cf. Varro, *de agric.* 2.10 (= *GARS* 150); Diodorus Siculus' account of the origins of the Sicilian slave rebellions, 34.2.27ff. (= *GARS* 229). Supervision was a major problem in a world where high status depended on landownership, yet implied participation in the political and social life of the urban *agora* or *forum*. Here too slavery provided a solution, by enabling the owner to be notionally in several places at once, through the person of a slave manager (*epitropos, vilicus*). Cf. M. H. Jameson, 'Agriculture and Slavery in Classical Athens', *CJ* 73 (1977/78), 122–45; R. Beare, 'Were Bailiffs ever Free-born?', *CQ* 28 (1978), 398–401.

5. D. Manacorda, 'The Ager Cosanus and the production of the Amphorae of Sestius', *JRS* 68 (1978), 122–31; D. W. Rathbone, 'The Development of Agriculture in the 'Ager Cosanus' during the Roman Republic: Problems of Evidence and Interpretation', *JRS* 71 (1981), 10–23; id., 'The Slave Mode of Production in Italy' (Review article), *JRS* 73 (1983), 160–68.

6. C. D. Goldin, *Urban Slavery in the American South 1820–1860* (Chicago, 1976).

7. R. H. Randall, 'The Erechtheum Workmen', *AJA* 57 (1953), 199–210; A. Burford, 'The Builders of the Parthenon', *Parthenos and Parthenon* (*G &R*, Suppl. vol. 10, 1963), 23–35.

8. T. B. L. Webster, *Potter and Patron in Classical Athens* (London, 1973); G. Prachner, *Die Sklaven und Freigelassene im arretinischen Sigillatagewerbe* (Wiesbaden, 1980); W. V. Harris, 'Roman Terracotta Lamps: the Organization of an Industry', *JRS* 70 (1980), 126–45; H. Tapio, *Organization of Roman Brick Production* (Helsinki, 1975).

9. E.g. Vogt, *Ancient Slavery*, chs. 5 and 6; J. Christes, *Sklaven und Freigelassene als Grammatiker und Philologen im antiken Rom* (Wiesbaden, 1979); J. Vogt, 'Nomenclator', *Gymnasium* 85 (1978), 327–38 = *Sklaverei und Humanität. Ergänzungsheft* (Wiesbaden, 1983), pp. 36ff.

10. R. Bogaert, *Banques et Banquiers dans les cités grecques* (Leiden, 1968); R. Veyne, 'Vie de Trimalcion', *Annales E.S.C.* 166 (1961), 213–47; J. H. D'Arms, *Commerce and Social Standing in Ancient Rome* (Cambridge, Mass., 1981): P. Garnsey, 'Independent Freedmen and the Economy of Roman Italy under the Principate', *Klio* 63 (1981), 359–71.

11. Most recently A. D. Booth, 'The Schooling of Slaves in First-Century Rome', *TAPhA* 109 (1979), 11–19.

12. Christes, n. 9 above.

13. Seneca, *Ep.* 27.5f. (= *GARS* 132).

14. J. Vogt, 'Alphabet für Freie und Sklaven', *Rh.Mus.* 116 (1973), 129–42 = *Sklaverei und Humanität. Ergänzungsheft* (Wiesbaden, 1983), pp. 17–27. But cf. Aristotle on a Syracusan slave-teacher: *Pol.* 1.2.22 (=*GARS* 2, p. 21).

15. S. Lauffer, *Die Bergwerkssklaven von Laureion* (Wiesbaden, 1979²); generally, J. F. Healy, *Mining and Metallurgy in the Greek and Roman World* (London, 1978). Despite more recent work, O. Davies, *Roman Mines in Europe* (Oxford, 1935), has not been superseded, and was reprinted in M. I. Finley's Ancient Economic History series (New York, 1979).

16. ILS 6891. D. Flach, 'Die Bergwerksordnungen von Vipasca', *Chiron* 9 (1979), 399–448.

17. I am aware of no modern monograph on *servi poenae*.

V. SLAVES IN PUBLIC SERVICE

The use of slaves, persons on the margins of society, in public service by both the Greeks and the Romans is at first sight a puzzle. There is no problem about an oriental monarch using 'slaves' to carry out his orders; the Persian kings treated their ministers as members of their household, and referred to them officially as their 'slaves'. That ordinary Persians should have to take orders from such 'slaves' was, in Greek eyes, a disgrace, and an essential feature of despotism. The use of slaves and freedmen by the Roman emperors, and of eunuch slaves – the extreme case of degradation – by the late imperial court, seemed to indicate Rome's decline from freedom to tyranny: for some modern writers, it was evidence that the Roman empire had turned into a typically oriental despotism. But this analysis only makes the use of slaves by Greek states, including Athens at its most democratic, and by the Roman republic, even more paradoxical.

The most accessible collection of material about slaves in state service at Athens remains that of O. Jacob.[1] Evidence about the use of slaves by other classical Greek cities is extremely sparse. Leaving aside servile agricultural workers directly or indirectly dependent upon the state like the Helots, it appears that state-owned slaves generally provided services, and were not engaged in production. The proposals made by various political philosophers and reformers for state-owned slaves to be employed as miners to increase state revenues[2] or as craftsmen to free all men of citizen status for agricultural work[3] suggest that the roles normally performed by Greek state-owned slaves were unlike those in an oriental despotism or in the Roman imperial household.

The services performed can be broadly divided into menial and managerial. There is no problem about explaining why at Athens the elected public officials responsible for keeping the city in good order, e.g., by removing corpses from public places (the ten *astynomoi*), or for looking after the roads (the five *hodopoioi*), should have had slaves to do their dirty work for them: as Aristotle pointed out, 'any community that is wealthy enough will appoint slaves to do these subordinate jobs'.[4] But the reasons for using slaves in responsible administrative positions were more complex. Inscriptions show that the Athenian democracy employed slaves (e.g.) to keep accounts of expenditure on behalf of the state, or to look after the official standards of weights and measures to ensure that they were not tampered with.[5] These men were what we call 'civil servants', and their task was to prevent free citizens from falsifying their expense accounts or

otherwise acting illegally. The importance of their job was recognized
by the relatively high allowance allocated to them (three obols a day,
while the maintenance allocated to a disabled citizen in the fourth
century B.C. was only two obols). Yet they remained slaves, and if
they failed in their duties the magistrates were required to punish
these 'civil servants' by whipping them, as was appropriate to slaves.

One explanation for this paradox is that the principles of the annual
rotation of office-holders, and of the distribution of responsibility
among various members of a board of magistrates which Greek states
considered essential to prevent the concentration of power in the
hands of a 'tyrant', made it difficult for essential technical information
to be transferred from one year's magistrates to the next. Continuity
had to be provided by subordinate administrators. Athens was a
democracy; had the permanent administration been staffed by citizens, it would have been impossible for them to avoid the political
and personal machinations of public life. Any citizen was linked to
some magistrate or ex-magistrate through family, tribal, or residential
ties; a state accountant could hardly control magisterial corruption if
he was firmly enmeshed in the same social nexus. Slaves were not of
course entirely without social bonds, but ideally those bonds tied them
only to their own master. If that master was not any individual but
the community itself, then (in theory) they could be expected to act
'objectively' as between one citizen and another.

One curious group of state slaves in classical Athens was the police,
a group of Scythians called 'archers' (*toxotai*). Their job, as depicted
in several Aristophanic comedies, was both menial and administrative;
hence slaves were ideal personnel. Citizens were not keen on a job
that involved 'unsocial hours' and physical danger, and was also likely
to bring one into conflict with those fellow-citizens whose activities
required policing. At the same time a policeman who had any kind of
social obligations towards the people he was trying to control might
well be open to corruption, and in the context of Athens' democratic
judicial system would certainly be unable to escape the suspicion of
corruption. State-owned slaves had no obligations to any individual
citizen, but only to their owner, the state. Using Scythians imported
from outside Athenian territory was intended to reinforce the ideal
absence of any links with particular citizens. Scythians were used as
policemen because they were outsiders, not because of their supposed
excellence as archers: the last thing they were expected to do was
shoot down errant citizens.

The literary, epigraphic, and legal sources for public slaves at Rome
are much fuller, and a great deal of work has been directed to them.
With the establishment of the Principate, slaves and freedmen of the

imperial household were inevitably called upon to perform functions which overlapped with those of 'state' slaves. The parallel functioning of gangs of state- and imperially-owned slaves is nicely illustrated by the co-existence of two slave families responsible for the maintenance of Rome's aqueducts, as described by Frontinus.[6]

There have been recent evaluations of the functions of state slaves in the strict sense in French and in German, including those slaves who looked after shrines in the care of the state.[7] A relatively un-explored field is that of municipally owned slaves in cities other than Rome, although some evidence, mainly papyrological, has come to light from Pompeii and elsewhere on the Bay of Naples. But most of the surviving testimony relates to the slaves of the imperial household; there is an excellent monograph in English on the *Familia Caesaris*.[8] The nature of the epigraphical evidence means that studies have inevit-ably tended to be biased towards those imperial slaves and (especially) freedmen who provided high-grade administrative services. There have been attempts to map out a regular career structure and to examine the role of imperial procurators as the managers of imperial resources in the form of both private estates and the *fiscus* of whole provinces.[9] There have been analyses of the services provided by some particular groups of slaves: the emperor's private bodyguard of Germans[10] and the women of the imperial household[11] have come under scrutiny. As is only to be expected, the emperor's *familia rustica* (agricultural slaves) has tended to escape attention simply because of the comparative absence of evidence.

In considering the *Familia Caesaris*, we are again faced with an apparent contradiction in the use of low-status individuals to perform high-status tasks. The feeling that there is something peculiar about this is not a modern one: Pliny and Tacitus, writing at a time when the top administrative positions were reserved to wealthy members of the equestrian order, were horrified at the power exercised by some of the freedmen-ministers of Julio-Claudian emperors, especially those of Claudius.[12] The abnormal power of these early imperial freedmen can be explained by the fact that the Principate had to be in existence for several generations before educated and wealthy men of free birth were prepared to compromise their 'freedom' by working for what was long regarded as the emperor's personal household.

By the end of the first century A.D. that particular prejudice had been overcome. But in the fourth century a parallel phenomenon developed, the rise of court eunuchs, as virulently condemned in contemporary literature as the freedmen of the Julio-Claudians had once been. Modern historiography tended for a long time to explain their influence in moral terms: 'Those unhappy beings, the ancient production of Oriental jealousy and despotism, were introduced into Greece and Rome by the contagion of Asiatic luxury.'[13] Recent studies have rejected such an explanation in terms of 'decadent' late Romans importing this and other degrading elements of Asiatic kingship. Some social historians have emphasized that eunuchs are even more closely dependent on their master than 'normal' slaves. The Roman ban on castration within the boundaries of the empire meant that any eunuch (in theory) had to come from outside. A eunuch's inability to produce offspring also guaranteed that, even when freed and thus able to hold high Palatine office, no eunuch would have any divided loyalties: there would be no wife whose family's interests had to be taken into account, no children whose career prospects had to be protected. Hence the eunuch was an ideal familiar for an emperor surrounded by potentially hostile military commanders and senatorial magnates.[14]

Patterson's Structuralist account of slavery provides a good explanation of the eunuch phenomenon.[15] While all slaves are 'marginal', imported eunuchs are extreme symbols of that marginality, since they are supposed to be unable to share in any human relationship of whatever kind. Consequently we find that in many societies eunuchs are associated with kings: in China and the Muslim world, as in the late Roman Empire, the ruler is the marginal mediator between human society and the divine, and it is appropriate that the man who guards entry from human society into the ruler's sacred presence should be a eunuch. This is neither characteristically 'oriental', nor morally decadent. In the *Acts of the Apostles* (8:27) a black eunuch who belongs to a female ruler illustrates how Christianity embraces all human society to its social as well as its geographical margins.

The use of slaves as soldiers by Greek and Roman communities raises further questions. As we have seen, it was entirely appropriate that slave personnel should have been used for policing duties at Athens; and it does not surprise that powerful Roman landowners should have had bands of slaves to enforce obedience on their tenants, or that Roman emperors used slaves to protect themselves against attack by their fellow-citizens. But what does contradict the classical world's clear distinction between citizen and slave is the use of slaves in what was the quintessential privilege of the free citizen, fighting. Slave soldiers such as those who dominated many medieval Muslim states[16] or slave rowers who serviced the Mediterranean war-galleys in the early modern period[17] were unthinkable so long as the citizen ideology of antiquity survived even in the most attenuated form.

The initial assumption must be that citizen-states as a rule made no use of slaves except in an auxiliary capacity.[18] But war is a stern teacher; and even the most successful military machine sometimes faced a manpower crisis, like the Athenians prior to Arginusae in 406 B.C. or the Romans after Cannae in 216 B.C. In such a situation, there was little hesitation in enrolling slaves as rowers or legionaries.[19] But they could not be enrolled as slaves: either they had to be manumitted first, or they were promised their freedom on condition that they fought well (it is not clear whether these promises were always kept). Almost all instances of slaves fighting can be explained as due to crises of this sort (there are some exceptions[20]). Those who saw themselves as legitimate rulers (including Aristonicus of Pergamum, see p. 41 below) thought that in extreme circumstances they had the right to promise slaves their freedom if they fought for them: hence slaves were manumitted by both sides in the Roman civil wars, praised as patriotic freedmen or condemned as fugitive criminals.[21]

NOTES

1. O. Jacob, *Les Esclaves Publics à Athènes* (Liège/Paris, 1928; repr. in M. I. Finley's Ancient Economic History series, New York, 1979). On services provided by slaves in Greek cities in the Hellenistic and Roman periods, cf. A. H. M. Jones, *The Greek City from Alexander to Justinian* (Oxford, 1940; repr. 1981), part IV.

2. Xen., *Poroi* 1.13–25 (= *GARS* 87).

3. Phaleas, ap. Arist., *Pol.* 2.4.13 (= *GARS* 159).

4. Arist., *Pol.* 4.12 (= *GARS* 158).

5. *IG* 2.1 No. 403 (= *GARS* 162) and *IG* 2.1 No. 476 (= *GARS* 163).

6. *GARS* 167.

7. N. Rouland, 'A propos des servi publici populi Romani', *Chiron* 7 (1977), 262–78; W. Eder, *Servitus Publica* (Wiesbaden, 1980).

8. P. R. C. Weaver, *Familia Caesaris* (Cambridge, 1972). Cf also F. Millar, *The Emperor in the Roman World* (London, 1977), esp. chs. 3 and 5.

9. Notably H. Chantraine, *Freigelassene und Sklaven im Dienst der römischen Kaiser. Studien zu ihrer Nomenklatur* (Wiesbaden, 1967); ibid., 'Ausserdienststellung und Altersversorgung kaiserlicher Sklaven und Freigelassener', *Chiron* 3 (1973), 307–29.

10. H. Bellen, *Die germanische Leibwache der römischen Kaiser des julisch-claudischen Hauses* (Wiesbaden, 1981).

11. J. Kolendo, 'Les femmes esclaves de l'empereur', *Actes du colloque 1973* (Paris, 1976), 399–416; S. Treggiari, 'Jobs in the Household of Livia', *PBSR* 43 (1975), 48–77.

12. Tacitus, *Ann.* 12.53 (= *GARS* 176); Pliny, *Ep.* 8.6. Cf. e.g. S. I. Oost, 'The Career of M. Antonius Pallas', *AJPh* 79 (1958), 11ff.

13. Gibbon, *Decline and Fall* I.19 and 32. Such judgments depend on taking a literal view of invectives such as Claudian's *In Eutropium*.

14. K. Hopkins, *Conquerors and Slaves* (Cambridge, 1978), ch. 3; P. Guyot, *Eunuchen als Sklaven und Freigelassene in der griechisch-römischen Antike* (Stuttgart, 1980).

15. Patterson, op. cit., pp. 315–31.

16. P. Crone, *Slaves on Horses* (Cambridge, 1980).

17. C. Verlinden, *L'Esclavage* (ch. II, no. 13 above), 1028ff.

18. Y. Garlan, *War in the Ancient World* (Engl. transl., London, 1975); K.-W. Welwei, *Unfreie im antiken Kriegsdienst*. I (Wiesbaden, 1974), II (1977), III (forthcoming); N. Rouland, *Les esclaves romaines en temps de guerre* (Brussels, 1977).

19. Arginusae: Xen., *Hell.* 1.6.24; after Chaeronea in 338 B.C.: Hypereides Fg.29 (= *GARS* 89); after Cannae, Val. Max. 7.6.1; Livy 22.57.11 (cf. *GARS* 58).

20. L. Casson, 'Galley Slaves', *TAPhA* 97 (1966), 35–44; on Polybius 10.17 (= *GARS* 114), J. M. Libourel, 'Galley Slaves in the Second Punic War', *CPh* 68 (1973), 116–19.

21. Augustus, *Res Gestae* 4.25 (= *GARS* 61); Suet., *Aug.* 16; Dio Cassius 48.19 (= *GARS* 59) and 49.12 (= *GARS* 60).

VI. DISCONTENT AND REBELLION

For most of the nineteenth century and up until recently, the slave rebellion has been one of the most important components of the educated public's image of life in the Greek and Roman world. Since the 1960's, academic scholars have come to see that there is little historical evidence to justify the traditional picture of slave societies as 'police states' constantly at the brink of violent rebellion, and that the frequency and scale of uprisings had been greatly over-emphasized.[1]

One reason for this overemphasis was the romantic nationalism that spread first with, and then in opposition to, the French Revolution; and its characteristic symbol has been the figure of Spartacus. The ancient accounts of the Spartacus war assisted the process, since alongside the expected hostile attitude towards him (to be found in Cicero and the Livian tradition), another group of sources treats him much more respectfully as Horace's 'Spartacus acer'.[2] Spartacus was thus sufficiently noble to qualify as a subject for eighteenth-century French tragedy. The plot of Bernard-Joseph Saurin's drama *Spartacus* of 1760 revolves around Crassus' daughter falling in love with him. Then – partly in reaction against Saurin's frivolous treatment – Spartacus was chosen by the dramatists Lessing (1727–81) and Grillparzer (1791–1872) to symbolize resistance against tyranny. Freemasons saw him as an Enlightenment hero in the struggle against 'Roman' Catholicism; and early nineteenth-century nationalism made Spartacus the liberator, not so much of slaves as a social class, as of the national groups enslaved by Rome.

Subsequently Spartacus was appropriated by Socialists as the symbol of class rather than national resistance. Social Democrats as well as Communists saw slave wars, and Spartacus' in particular, as the most important phenomenon in ancient history.[3] Karl Liebknecht and Rosa Luxemburg, the organizers of German communism, named their revolutionary movement and their journal (1916) after him. After the theory of the 'five stages' of world history had attained the status of orthodoxy in the Soviet Union, Spartacus became as divine a figure as Stalin himself. As late as the 1960's, Soviet school books portrayed the dying Spartacus as a substitute for Christ crucified (plate no. 8). Other leaders of slave rebellions were similarly honoured. At the height of the Cold War, the city council of Enna in Sicily erected a statue to Eunus proudly proclaiming that his Sicilian slave rebellion had taken place 'two thousand years before Abraham Lincoln'. Even some scholars who were not Socialists were inclined to believe that there was some sort of 'Red International' orchestrating the two Sicilian revolts of ca. 135–32 and 104–100 B.C., Aristonicus of Pergamum's war against Rome (133–129), the uprising at Laureum in Attica in ca. 102 B.C., and the Spartacus war (73–71).

In a major article first published in 1957, Joseph Vogt showed that these slave rebellions could not be understood in terms of such a uniform scheme. The causes and the course of each rebellion had to be seen individually; even if the resentment felt by slaves everywhere was heightened by the general social conditions of Italy and Sicily in the late republic, that resentment only turned to violence as a result of peculiar conditions at particular times and places. In a further paper Vogt demonstrated that just because slaves were invited to participate in Aristonicus' war against Rome, it did not follow that this war was in any real sense a slave rebellion.[4] Although the conclusion that had to be drawn from Vogt's empirical study of the evidence met with resistance from scholars behind the Iron Curtain, Eastern European Marxists have recently become willing to accept that rebellions were exceptional events. This admission need not affect the picture of 'class struggle' in antiquity, except that the emphasis must be on less spectacular ways in which slaves resisted the extraction of surplus value by slave-owners: sleeping on the job, drinking, petty pilfering, and in the last resort running away.[5] Marxists continue to be interested in rebellions against the Roman government by servile groups in Late Antiquity, though it is generally recognized that these were not chattel-slaves, but those groups destined to become the serfs of the new 'Feudal Mode of Production'.[6] Particular attempts by some slaves to use force to attain their freedom (and to enslave others) cannot be held to imply any desire, organized or spontaneous, to abolish slavery as an institution.

The realization that rebellion is the exception and not the rule in slave societies has caused ideological problems for western liberals too. People who take individual freedom for granted find it difficult to appreciate why, for much of human history, social groups have been ready to put up with inferiority and lack of freedom. Considerable scholarly effort continues to be devoted to slave rebellions, and to the extent to which slaves joined wars and uprisings which were not initiated by slaves.[7]

This emphasis on violent resistance runs the risk of masking the fact that most slaves, most of the time, accepted their situation. That does not mean that rebellions are not particularly interesting as one of the few political phenomena actually brought about by slaves in a slaveholding society. It should be remembered, however, that all surviving accounts of slave insurrections were written by men of the citizen class, and that even when they have favourable things to say about the rebels, that may be for reasons to do with the political or intellectual concerns of free citizens. Posidonius' sympathetic account of the plight of Sicilian slaves, as excerpted by Diodorus Siculus, can only be understood in the context of the philosopher's Stoic views on personal behaviour (by slave owners) and on good government (by Rome); the positive ancient image of Spartacus may be traced back to Crassus' need to build Spartacus up as a worthy enemy, comparable to the Sertorius recently defeated by his rival Pompey.

A more promising line of enquiry is to examine slave rebellions in terms of recent sociological studies of banditry. In both the modern Americas and the ancient Mediterranean, minor rebellions by groups of fugitive slaves might be so successful that they were, at least temporarily, tolerated by the authorities. Although for Antiquity far less evidence survives about such bands than about the more spectacular slave rebellions, it is easy to see that the stories told (e.g.) about the fugitives Drimacus of Chios or Felix Bulla fit this pattern. Again it is clear that while such banditry led to the freeing of particular slaves, it did not aim to free (existing) slaves in general, let alone at the abolition of slavery as such.[8]

The demotion of slave rebellions as the extreme manifestation of 'class warfare' has led to a search for evidence of a permanent state of hostility in other aspects of slave behaviour. In particular, the more extreme provisions of Roman law regarding the return of fugitive slaves or the execution of all those slaves present in their master's house if he died a violent death (the *Senatusconsultum Silanianum*) have been seen as evidence of permanent fear of slave resistance by their owners, confirmed by Seneca's quip 'Every slave is an enemy'.[9] Such a view may be valid for those Greek states in which the citizen community lorded it over servile subject-communities. Plutarch believed that in ancient Sparta the Ephors had formally declared war on the Helots each year in order to legitimate any killings of Helots that might occur.[10] But many scholars, including some Marxists, would now accept that this cannot be applied to the relationship between chattel-slaves, even those in agriculture, and the free community.

Needless to say, the resentment that individual slaves felt towards the masters they had to serve did manifest itself in violence on occasions (as did that of masters towards their slaves; not to mention husbands/wives, parents/children, teachers/pupils throughout human history). While cases of slaves murdering their masters, laying a curse on them, or simply running away, are frequently referred to by scholars in general discussions of ancient slavery, there have been

surprisingly few systematic studies of these phenomena. Heinz
Bellen's work on fugitives in the Roman empire is an exception.[11]
Earlier studies, including several by Italian jurists, tended to concen-
trate on the wide range of problems that runaways caused for Roman
law (e.g., who was responsible for a fugitive slave's delicts, who
owned his 'property'). Interest persists in the methods used to control
potential runaways and other recalcitrant slaves: the 'ergastulum' for
farm workers;[12] for others, branding and, especially after Constantine
banned branding on the face on religious grounds, slave collars.
These individual studies confirm that in both Greece and Rome
fugitive slaves were a major problem for slave-owners at all times. In
particular circumstances, such as the Spartan occupation of Attica
during the Decelean war, Alexander's long-distance campaigns in Asia
(which led to soldiers' taking out an insurance policy in case their
slaves decamped), or the civil wars of the late Republic, owners'
control over their slaves was so weak that the problem became particularly acute.[13] But literary and epigraphical sources make it clear
that it was a constant problem everywhere and at every period, whatever the numbers or proportion of slaves in a community. Hence all
states had to take cognizance of the fact that some slaves could not
put up with their particular masters; and it is clear that many if not
all ancient communities recognized that if a slave had indeed been
badly treated, he had the right to take refuge at a religious shrine, or
later at the statue of a Roman emperor or in a Christian church. This
would give religious or secular authorities an opportunity either to
reconcile master and slave, or, if things had gone too far for that, to
arrange for the slave to be sold to another master with whom he
might get on better (that master might be a temple-god). I. M. Lewis'
study of *Ecstatic Religion*[14] demonstrates how in other cultures social
groups with few or no legal rights express their opposition to the way
their social superiors are treating them by appealing to the divine
world. This enables the dominant individuals to stop behaving op-
pressively without abandoning the principle that they had the right to
behave as they did; for they are not giving way to an inferior, but to
the divinity to whom that inferior has appealed. Our ancient sources
make it clear that slaves were particularly ready to appeal to the divine
world for help, through prayers, curses, and flight to places of
asylum.[15] This was not because they and other inferior social groups
like women were less 'rational' than the men who constituted the
society of citizens, but because their lack of legal and political rights
meant that the only way they could seek redress for injustice was by
appealing to the divine.

NOTES

1. Cf. especially S. Elkins, *Slavery* (Chicago, 1959). Slave revolts were considerably more common in Latin America and the Caribbean, where a greater proportion of slaves were recent arrivals from Africa.

2. Horace, *Ep.* 16.5 and *C.*4. 14.19; G. Stampacchia, 'Spartacus Acer', *Klio* 63 (1981), 331–46; M. A. Levi, 'La Tradizione sul Bellum Servile di Spartaco', *Actes du colloque 1971* (Paris, 1972), 171–4.

3. There are dozens of works, academic and popular, on Spartacus, but comparatively few in English. Cf. B. Baldwin, 'Two Aspects of the Spartacus Slave Revolt', *CJ* 62 (1966), 289–94; A. Guarino, *Spartaco. Analysi di un mito* (Naples, 1979) = *Spartakus* (German transl., Munich, 1980); R. Günther, *Der Aufstand des Spartakus* (Berlin East, 1979, and Cologne, 1980).

4. J. Vogt, 'The Structure of Ancient Slave Wars' and 'Pergamum and Aristonicus', *Ancient Slavery*, chs. 3 & 4.

5. K. R. Bradley, *Slaves and Masters*, pp. 26–33.

6. Mostly in Russian; but cf. H. J. Diesner, 'Das römische Imperium und der Freiheitskampf der Unterdrückten im Westen des römischen Reiches', in *Humanismus und Menschenbild im Orient und in der Antike* (Wiss. Beiträge, Halle, 1977), pp. 69–77. E. A. Thompson, 'Peasant Revolts' (ch. I, n. 9 above) is a Marxist classic.

7. K. R. Bradley, 'Slaves and the Conspiracy of Catiline', *CPh* 73 (1978), 329–36; Z. Rubinsohn, 'Was the Bellum Spartacium a Servile Insurrection?', *Riv.Fil.* 99 (1971), 290–299; W. Hoben, *Terminologische Studien zu den Sklavenerhebungen der römischen Republik* (Wiesbaden, 1978).

8. J. Vogt, 'Zum Experiment des Drimakos: Sklavenhaltung und Räuberstand', *Saeculum* 24 (1973), 213–19 = *Sklaverei und Humanität. Ergänzungsheft* (Wiesbaden, 1983), pp. 28ff.; A. Fuks, 'Slave War and Slave Troubles in Chios in the Third Century B.C.', *Athenaeum* 46 (1968), 102ff.

9. Seneca, *Ep.* 47.5; but he goes on to say, 'we do not acquire them as enemies: we make them our enemies'. On Tac., *Ann.* 14.42.5, I. Kajanto, 'Tacitus on the Slaves', *Arctos* 6 (1970), 43–60; H. Bellen, 'Antike Staatsräson', *Gymnasium* 89 (1982), 449–67.

10. Plut., *Lyk.* 28, quoting Aristotle.

11. H. Bellen, *Studien zur Sklavenflucht im römischen Kaiserreich* (Wiesbaden, 1971).

12. J. C. Fitzgibbon, 'Ergastula', *Classical News and Views* (Ottawa), 20 (1976), 55–9.

13. Thuc. 7.27 (= *GARS* 211); Arist., *Oik.* 2.2.34 (= *GARS* 217); Augustus, *Res Gestae* 4.25 (= *GARS* 61). Cf. M. Hadas, 'Vestal Virgins and Runaway Slaves', *CW* 24 (1931), 108.

14. I. M. Lewis, *Ecstatic Religion* (Harmondsworth, 1971).

15. A comprehensive study of slaves' participation in ancient religious cults was compiled by F. Bömer, *Untersuchungen über die Religion der Sklaven in Griechenland und Rom*, I–IV (Wiesbaden, 1957–63).

On Christianity and slavery, see ch. II, n. 12 above.

I wish to thank Professor Keith Hopkins for his comments on an early draft of this survey and Dr E. Herrmann of the Mainz Academy for providing me with material not available in Bristol.

ADDENDA (1992)

The Pattern of Research since 1987

The 1980's saw the sudden collapse of communism in Eastern Europe, and in the West the equally unexpected acceptance of the free-market values associated with the policies of Reagan and Thatcher. While many scholars continue to believe that their research is, or should be, free of external constraints, they have inevitably been affected by the changed institutional conditions under which they work, as well as new intellectual patterns in the wider world.

The clearest way in which approaches to ancient slavery have been affected by these changes in the last few years is that Marxism can no longer serve to provide either a convincing or a coherent framework for economic historians. When W. Z. Rubinsohn wrote *Spartacus' Uprising and Soviet Historical Writing* in 1983, the abuse of slavery and slave rebellions by communist regimes was frightening; a forthcoming account of the Spartacus myth since the eighteenth century can represent its exploitation as frequently verging on the ridiculous.[1] No European regime any longer forces its scholars to produce politically orthodox studies of ancient slavery. But serious students of antiquity, including Marxists, had already seen by the 1970's that the mechanisms by which élites abstracted surplus wealth from others could not be reduced to the slave/ slaveowner (let alone the slave/citizen) polarity espoused by classical Marxists, notwithstanding the prominence of that polarity in our Greek and Latin sources. The emphasis has shifted to other inequalities: between landlord and tenant, government official and subject, and within the household between middle-aged and young, and particularly male and female workers. The global studies of ancient slavery by French and Italian scholars represent the last fling of Marxism.[2] Elsewhere even Marxists now discuss slavery only as one aspect of a wider economic context, either in theoretical discussions[3] or discursive narratives.[4] Analyses of ancient agricultural practices award slavery only a limited role.[5] These studies also reveal the importance now ascribed to quantification (in step with the importance of accountants in the wider world?). Cambridge scholars in particular, while continuing to profess loyalty to the inspiration of M. I. Finley,[6] have produced macro-economic studies in which slavery only occurs incidentally.[7] Others prove that where reliable records exist, slavery can be shown to have been only one (minor) element in economic life, as in an important recent study of agricultural production on one particular estate in Egypt, based on the hard evidence of papyrus documents.[8] But as the continuing controversy about the number of slaves at Athens illustrates,[9] the nature of the source material for antiquity – the fact that there rarely ever was any real information about the economy collected at any level above that of the individual household – limits the extent to which those disposed to quantify can produce reliable conclusions about precise 'numbers', whether as costs, profits, or prices (e.g., the price of slaves on the notional 'slave-market'). Another topic which is becoming academically respectable is banking, though again slaves and freedmen occur only incidentally.[10]

Social historians, too, have distanced themselves from granting slavery the privileged position it was accorded in the previous twenty years. A more balanced picture has emerged, with slaves being seen in the social context of other groups: the old,[11] the young (including children),[12] and especially women.[13] In the context of family and household, slaves can be only one part of the marginalized group as a whole, and studies of them specifically are relatively few. To generalize, the specific study of slavery has given way to that of the private household and the family.[14] Progressive academics have abandoned the study of 'class' in favour of that of gender. This has produced work on the sexual exploitation of slaves, but again only in the context of the history of sexual exploitation (male and female) generally.[15]

A number of factors have therefore conspired to turn the spotlight away from slavery. In addition, the increasing burden of administration and teaching loads on academics, coupled with the imperative to publish (quantitatively) more and more, has also perhaps meant that time-consuming searches through literary or material remains have, in the English-speaking world, tended to suffer at the expense of re-interpretations requiring new thinking rather than original research. Rather, there have been surveys summarizing earlier work, for instance on slave-rebellions.[16] The need for newer, perhaps simpler student textbooks has resulted in surveys (not excluding this one), normally aiming to inform students of the state-of-play rather than at radical re-interpretations.[17]

But the bottom has not completely fallen out of the slavery market. Original research continues, especially under the auspices of the Mainz Academy.[18] One notable aspect of work on slavery in the last decade has been the attention given to Roman law, previously very much an underused source of information about slavery (see my comment on p. 20). Some of these studies are specific to slavery, most significantly Alan Watson's survey of *Roman Slave Law* and W. Waldstein's discussion of the economic obligations of freed slaves.[19] Other studies have dealt with *servi poenae* and imprisonment, branding, adoption, Junian Latins, and imperial restrictions on prostituting slaves.[20] Again, important points about Roman slavery are often made only incidentally in legal studies; a fascinating recent book on Roman wills includes a relevant chapter on 'servants and friends'.[21]

The connection between slavery and early Christianity continues to excite interest. While the consensus amongst ancient historians is now that early Christians were not noticeably poorer or 'lower class', there is a striking connection between Christianity and freedmen, especially those of the imperial *familia.* The Harvard sociologist Orlando Patterson gives this factor a prominent place in the first volume of an analysis of freedom, less convincing in its 'politically correct' claim that women were constantly associated with slaves in the struggle for different kinds of freedom in antiquity.[22]

NOTES

1. Z. Rubinsohn: translated J. G. Griffith (Oxford, 1987); A. J. L. van Hooff on Spartacus (Nijmegen, 1992; in Dutch).

2. Y. Garlan, *Les esclaves en Grèce ancienne* (Paris, 1982: reviewed in *CR* 33 (1983), 265–7) appeared as a paperback in English as late as 1988 (*Slavery in Ancient Greece*, Cornell U.P.); J. C. Dumont, *Servus: Rome et l'esclavage sous la république* (Ecole Française de Rome, 1987); the three volumes on Settefinestre edited by A. Carandini and A. Ricci, *Settefinestre: una villa schiavistica nell' Etruria Romana* (Modena, 1985: rev. *JRS* 78 (1988), 194ff.) were followed by A. Carandini, *Schiavi in Italia* (Rome, 1988: rev. *JRS* 80 (1990), 195f.); see also C. Wickham, 'Marx, Sherlock Holmes, and Late Roman Commerce', review article, *JRS* 78 (1988), 183ff., for a discussion of the traditional Marxist approach of the end of slavery. It remains to be seen whether the Gramsci Institute, founded in Rome in 1974, will continue to further the study of ancient slavery. The Besançon centre founded by Pierre Lévêque (p. 10, n. 19) widened its horizons from the early 1980's.

3. J. R. Love, *Antiquity and Capitalism* (Routledge, 1991).

4. G. E. M. de Ste. Croix, *The Class Struggle in the Ancient Greek World* (Duckworth, 1981).

5. In Britain the move away from slavery began with the International Economic History Conference in Edinburgh in 1978, where the Ancient History section discussed non-slave labour; see P. Garnsey (ed.), *Non-Slave Labour in the Greco-Roman World* (Cambridge, 1980). More recent work includes: E. M. Wood, *Peasant Citizen and Slave* (Verso, 1988); L. Foxhall, 'The Dependent Tenant: Land Leasing and Labour in Italy and Greece', *JRS* 80 (1990), 97ff.; T. W. Gallant, *Risk and Survival in Ancient Greece* (Cambridge, 1991); R. Sallares, *The Ecology of the Ancient Greek World* (London, 1991).

6. M. I. Finley (ed.), *Classical Slavery* (London, 1987).

7. P. D. A. Garnsey, *Famine and Food Supply in the Graeco-Roman World* (Cambridge, 1988); C. R. Whittaker (ed.), *Pastoral Economies in Classical Antiquity* (Cambridge, 1988); R. Duncan-Jones, *Structure and Scale in the Roman Economy* (Cambridge, 1990).

8. D. Rathbone, *Economic rationalism and rural society in third-century Egypt. The Heroninus archive and the Appianus estate* (Cambridge, 1991).

9. Wood, Sallares pp. 53–60 (n. 5 above).

10. J. Andreau, *La Vie Financière* (Ecole Française de Rome, 1987), on professional (mainly freedmen) bankers; A. Kirschenbaum, *Sons, Slaves and Freedmen in Roman Commerce* (Jerusalem, 1987); see p. 40, n. 10.

11. As recent bibliographies of old age show, virtually no work has been done on old slaves. Cf. W. Suder, *Geras* (Wroclaw, 1991); J.-U. Krause, *Die Familie und weitere anthropologische Grundlagen.* (Bibliographie zur römischen Sozialgeschichte 1. Habes 11; Stuttgart, 1992). The chapters on antiquity in G. Minois, *History of Old Age* (Polity Press, 1989) show how much remains to be done. Old age was advertised as one of the topics for the German-language Mommsen-society conference in 1993, but the response appears to have been disappointing.

12. M. Golden, *Children and Childhood in Classical Athens* (Johns Hopkins, 1990).

13. S. Dixon, *The Roman Mother* (1988); G. Clark, *Women in the Ancient World* (*Greece & Rome* New Surveys in the Classics, No. 21, Oxford, 1989); R. Günther, *Frauenarbeit – Frauenbindung* (Historisches Institut Mannheim; Munich, 1987), rev. *JRS* 79 (1989), 228f.; *Helios*, vol. 16 (1989); S. Treggiari, *Roman Marriage* (Oxford, 1991).

14. P. Veyne, *History of Private Life* (English translation, 1987); D. I. Kertzer and R. P. Saller, *The Family in Italy from Antiquity to the Present* (Yale, 1991); K. R. Bradley, *Discovering the Roman Family* (Oxford, 1991), with chapters on child-labour and childcare; wet-nursing in B. Rawson (ed.), *The Family in Ancient Rome* (1986), which also has a piece on status in 'mixed marriages' by P. R. C. Weaver, 145ff.; B. Rawson (ed.), *Marriage, Divorce and Children in Ancient Rome* (Routledge, 1991), where chapters 7 and 8 on authority and the children of freed slaves are relevant.

15. T. A. J. McGinn, 'Taxation of Roman Prostitutes', *Helios* 16, 1 (1989) (based on a Madison dissertation, 1986); D. Halperin, *One Hundred Years of Homosexuality* (New York/London, 1990), ch. 5; D. Cohen, *Law, Sexuality and Society* (Cambridge, 1991), on Athens.

16. K. Bradley, *Slavery and Rebellion in the Roman World* (Batsford, 1989).

17. N. Fisher, *Slavery in Ancient Greece* ('Inside the Ancient World' series, BCP, forthcoming); G. Alföldy, *Antike Sklaverei* (Bamberg, 1988); and more substantially I. Biezunska Malowist, *La Schiavitù nel Mondo Antico* (Napoli, 1991).

18. R. Klein, *Die Sklaverei in der Sicht der Bischöfe Ambrosius und Augustinus* (Mainz Forschungen xx, 1988); K.-W. Welwei, *Unfreie im antiken Kriegsdienst*, 3: Rom (xxi, 1988); a revision of H. Volkmann, *Massenversklavungen* (xxii, 1990); R. Scholl, *Corpus der ptolemäischen Sklaventexte* (Beiheft, 1990); E. Herrmann-Otto, *Ex Ancilla Natus* (on *vernae*), forthcoming. Work on translating East European (Marxist) works continues for the time being; E. M. Staerman and others, *Die Sklaverei in den westlichen Provinzen des römischen Reiches im 1.–3. Jahrhundert* (Mainz Academy, 1987), with the corresponding volume on slavery in the eastern provinces appearing in late 1992. The bibliography continues to be updated, and a compendium ('Handwörterbuch der antiken Sklaverei') is in course of preparation. For a survey of the Academy's work, see H. Bellen, *Die antike Sklaverei als moderne Herausforderung* (Mainz Academy, 1989: the title is an implicit response to Finley's intemperate attack in *Ancient Slavery and Modern Ideology*: p. 10, n. 18 above).

19. A. Watson, *Roman Slave Law* (Johns Hopkins, 1987); W. Waldstein, *Operae Libertorum* (Mainz Forschungen xix, 1986: rev. *CR* 38 (1988), 331–3.).

20. On p. 40, n. 15 above, I should have mentioned F. Millar, 'Condemnation to Hard Labour in the Roman Empire', *PBSR* 52 (1984), 124 ff; cf. A. Burden, in: L. Archer (ed.), *Slavery and Other Forms of Unfree Labour* (Routledge, 1988); C. P. Jones, 'Stigma', *JRS* 77 (1987), 139 ff.; J. Gardner, 'Julia's Freedmen. Questions of Law and Status', *BICS* 35 (1988), 94 ff.; ibid., 'The Adoption of Roman Freedmen', *Phoenix* 43 (1989), 236 ff.; and her forthcoming *Being a Roman Citizen* (Routledge, 1993); P. R. C. Weaver, 'Where have all the Junian Latins gone? Nomenclature and status in the Early Empire', *Chiron* 20 (1990), 275 ff.; A. Sicari, *Prostituzione e tutela giuridica della schiava* (Bari, 1991).

21. E. Champlin, *Final Judgements* (California, 1991), ch. 7.

22. D. J. Kyrtatas, *The Social Structure of the Early Christian Communities* (London, 1987); O. Patterson, *Freedom in the Making of Western Culture* (Tauris Press, 1991). For accounts of the 'end' of slavery in late antiquity, see Wickham (n. 2 above).